Storm Clouds
over
Cyprus

A Briefing

Clement Dodd

Eothen
Huntingdon, Cambridgeshire

British Library Cataloguing-in-Publication Data.
A catalogue record for this book is available from the British
Library.

Published 2001.
© Clement Dodd, 2001.

Published by The Eothen Press, 10 Manor Road, Hemingford
Grey, Huntingdon, Cambridgeshire, England, PE28 9BX.

ISBN 0906719 32 1

It is better to light a candle than
to curse the darkness.

MAP OF CYPRUS

Dipkarpaz

Famagusta (*Gazimağusa*)
Varosha (*Maraş*)

Dhekelia
Base

Geçitkale

Ercan

Pyla

Larnaca

Kyrenia (*Girne*)

500m

NICOSIA
(*LEFKOŞA*)

Lefkara

Güzelyurt
(*Morphou*)

Limassol

Lefke

Akrotiri
Base

500

1000

Troodos

500

Erenköy

1000

Paphos

500

30 km
20 miles

N

UK Sovereign Base area

Airport

Contents

Preface

The Cyprus dispute could well lead to a dangerous instability in the Eastern Mediterranean in the next few years that will mainly affect Europe and the Middle East.

This briefing is intended for those who wish to get to the heart of the problem in as short a compass as possible. It is hoped that this brief account will be of help in the understanding of this dispute for politicians, officials, journalists and all those interested in the dispute and its impact on the region and beyond.

This booklet is based on the work of many students of the Cyprus issue as well as on my own research. I greatly regret that in so brief an analysis the contributions of others cannot be acknowledged. There is a particular debt that I would like to acknowledge, however, that to Christopher Brewin, who kindly read the manuscript.

A particular difficulty about writing on the subject of the Cyprus conflict is that each side refuses to accept the legality and legitimacy of the other, and consequently of the titles they use. My way out of this problem is to use the titles each side uses of itself. This may be regarded as offensive by both sides, for which I apologise since no offence is intended, but at least it is equal treatment.

A short reading list of general books has been added from which the reader will be able to explore further.

Clement Dodd

February 2001

| 1 |

Introduction

The Cyprus issue has been with us at least since 1963, but has much longer roots in history. It is an example of what has become a prime political problem of the modern world. Within any country does an ethnic, religious or otherwise distinguishable majority of the populace have the right to rule over all, including over a minority that wishes to rule itself? To a degree the answer must depend on the size, history and nature of the minority, questions to be explored later in this briefing.

For the present the important fact is that the two communities of Greek and Turkish Cypriots have been geographically separate since 1974, when the Turkish Government intervened militarily in the island and thus allowed for the emergence of a separate Turkish Cypriot state, which is still not recognised by any country save Turkey.

As a result it is still not possible generally speaking to cross from one side of the divide to the other. The Turkish Cypriot authorities would allow free movement of tourists from the South to the North, but the South will only allow one day visits. The United Nations forces may move across the dividing line, but are restricted to certain points and have to pay taxes and other dues to the North. Foreigners with houses in the North that were not Greek owned before 1974 usually may cross over the border, provided they did not enter Cyprus via the North. Journalists from both sides have some degree of access, as do political party leaders. In particular, left-wing party groups meet quite frequently at the Ledra Palace, a former hotel on the border in Nicosia taken over by the United Nations.

There is on the border one mixed village, Pile, where relations between the two sides can range from the friendly to the fragile. Also from time to time quite a number of Turkish Cypriots go informally to work in the South on a daily basis.

Size and population
The island is about half the size of Wales, or seven tenths the size of Connecticut. At its nearest point it is some 40 miles from Turkey. The distance to Greece is 500 miles. The South comprises 63 per cent of the island and includes the border zone manned by UN forces. There are two British sovereign bases on the island, Akrotiri and Dhekalia, occupying in total about ninety-nine square miles. They are listening and staging posts; there are more listening facilities elsewhere in the South on sites leased from the Greek Cypriot Government.

The population of the South is much greater than that of the North. The South has some 664,000 inhabitants, of whom 641,000 are Greek Cypriots, the remainder being Maronites, Armenians, Latins and a wide variety of foreigners, including many domestic workers. The population of the North is some 200,000, according to a December 1996 census.

When the then 12,000 Turkish and other foreign students, and the families of Turkish military officers, are deducted, the truly resident population was just over 180,000. Of these the census showed that at most some 40,000 were born in Turkey. They will mainly be 'settlers' on agricultural land who came from Turkey in the years following 1974, but the figure will include other workers in various trades and professions. The Greek Cypriots do not accept these figures.

They estimate the numbers of 'settlers' to be as high as half, or more than half, the population. There seems to be no solid basis for these figures, which nevertheless tend to be accepted uncritically by the UN and other international organisations. Since they do not recognise the North it seems that they are averse to using its statistics, published though they are.

The economies
Economically the Greek Cypriots are much better off than the Turkish Cypriots, with a per capita of $13,500, as compared with $4,200 for the North. However, the North is not as poor as the official figures suggest. For instance, in recent years there has been a significant increase in vehicle registrations. There has also been a great deal of new building, and in the villages everywhere homes are being improved and extended. The last few years have also seen the widespread purchase of television sets, washing machines and other 'white goods'. In addition to Turkish economic aid, one reason for the North's relative recent prosperity has been, no doubt, the development of the five universities, teaching in English, which draw students very largely from Turkey. Visits by their families, and by Turks who come to take advantage of the many casinos in the North, boost tourism. International tourism is greatly restricted by the international embargo on direct flights to the North. Private capital for building is coming in from Turkey and from Turkish Cypriots who have prospered abroad.

All this boosts an economy that was not allowed in 1994, by decision of the European Court, to export to any state in the European Union. This is regarded as right by Greek Cypriots on the grounds that resources from which the exports were being generated belong to them. They also claim that the principal reason for the relative poverty of the North, is not the international embargo: they tend to ascribe it to public corruption, inefficiency and a traditional Turkish lack of a capacity for enterprise (which is not borne out in Turkey any longer).

With a weak economy the North relies greatly on Turkey. The revenue raised by the government covers only about two-thirds of expenditure, the budget being balanced by the Turkish Government. In addition Ankara has provided capital for major infra-structural developments: roads, power installations, telecommunications, ports and airports have all been developed.

Government and politics
The political system of the South is based on an amended version of the 1960 Constitution. There is a single legislature of 56 members, elected now through a system of proportional representation. A further 24 seats are reserved for the 'absent' Turkish Cypriots. These seats have been vacant since 1963.

The system is presidential, the directly elected president constituting the executive power. The management of foreign affairs is generally within the remit of the president. Major legislation has to be approved by the House of Representatives, but may be proposed by ministers. These ministers are the members of the executive Council chosen by the president, but they cannot also be members of the House of Representatives.

The term of the present president, Glafcos Clerides, ends in 2003, but elections for the legislature to be held in May 2001 could bring about his resignation since, to be effective, the president has to have sufficient support in the House of Representatives. He is supported by the moderately nationalist and right-wing Democratic Rally (DESY), by the small United Democrats Party (EDE) led by George Vassiliou and by some members of the more nationalist Democratic Party (DEKO). This party led, till recently, by one of the hard men of Greek Cypriot politics, Spyros Kyprianou, is little inclined to make concessions to the Turkish Cypriots, and has about 12 per cent support among the population. The other hard-line party, the Socialist Party (EDEK) led by Vassos Lyssarides, also has about 12 per cent support. The moderate right DESY and the Reform Party of the Working People (AKEL) led by Demetrios Chrisofias, each obtain about 35 per cent support. They are both prepared to make concessions to obtain a settlement with the Turkish Cypriots, though they are not at all happy about sharing power with them on an equal basis. This reflects majority feeling in the South. At the last presidential election a candidate supported chiefly by AKEL came very close to winning. There is therefore just the possibility that either as a result of parliamentary elections in 2001, or of the presidential election in 2003, a government might emerge rather more inclined to make concessions in negotiations.

In the North the regime is parliamentary. Members are elected through a system of proportional representation. The government is formed from the National Assembly in the way usual in parliamentary systems. The president of the republic is elected by popular vote, but does not head the government, unlike the president in the South. The head of the government is the prime minister, at present, Derviş Eroğlu. Nevertheless, by virtue of his experience and standing the president, Rauf Denktash, virtually controls negotiations on the Cyprus issue. Eroğlu heads the National Unity Party, nationalist in a pro-Turkish sense and right-wing, and founded after 1974 by Denktash. The latter's son was until recently head of the more moderate Democratic Party which broke away from the National Unity Party. On the left is, first, the moderate left-wing Communal Liberation Party under Mustafa Akıncı, now in uneasy coalition with the dominant National Unity Party. Further left is the Republican Turkish Party under Mehmet Ali Talat.

The National Unity Party is the strongest by far, gaining over 40 per cent of the vote in the 1998 parliamentary elections, followed by the Democratic Party with some 22 per cent. Of the left-wing parties, who are more inclined to make concessions to the Greek Cypriots, the CLP obtained 15 per cent and the RTP only 13 per cent. The latter has the closest relations with the Greek Cypriots, partiularly with AKEL.The solidity of the nationalist right was confirmed in the presidential elections held in April 2000 when Denktash won almost 44 per cent of the vote and Eroğlu 30 per cent, the latter conceding defeat, declining a second run-off ballot. Eroğlu is rather less inclined to be conciliatory to the Greek Cypriots than Denktash, but their positions on the Cyprus issue are almost identical. Friction does arise from time to time between president and prime minister, but mainly on other issues.

The solidity of popular support for a firm policy on the Cyprus issue was somewhat shaken in the summer of 2000 when the collapse of some banks, and the government's determination, prompted by Ankara, to introduce a stringent packet of measures to control government expenditure more effectively, sparked off demonstrations against the government and against President Denktash. The left-wing protested against domination by Ankara and urged more emphasis on agreement with the South for a settlement that would allow the relatively impoverished North to benefit from the financial largesse of the European Union. Turkey has recently promoted a new Action Plan designed to help the North's economy further, but restrictions on early retirement, the taxation of pensions and other similar measures have not been accepted without protest. Further planned economic integration with Turkey is well-nigh inevitable, but is not welcomed by many Turkish Cypriots. The control of all Turkish and Turkish Cypriot forces by a Turkish general, and Turkish control of the police are also seriously questioned by the opposition. The president has expressed the view that if the police were controlled by the government, they would become politicised. In small societies it probably is better to have the administration under the control of the president in a presidential system.

| 2 |

A Living History

For the Greek and Turkish Cypriots their history is more than the record of a dead past. History inspires and justifies their present claims. In their schools it is a vital part of the curriculum.

The year 1974 is a year of grievous memory for the Greek Cypriots; for the Turkish Cypriots the year of bitter memory is 1963. The 'invasion', which for the Turkish Cypriots was the 'peace operation', was justified by Ankara as a military intervention by a Guarantor Power under authority of the 1960 Treaty of Guarantee. Initial international reaction was not unfavourable.

Intervention by Turkey was a great shock for the Greek Cypriots. Many had thought that the United States would never allow it to happen. They lost their control over Cyprus, being left with only 63 per cent of the island. Some 150,000 Greek Cypriots took flight to the South, many fearful for their lives. For the Turkish Cypriots it was rough justice: it was retribution for their sufferings between 1963 to 1974 under Greek Cypriot rule when more than half took refuge from Greek Cypriot violence by defending themselves in tiny fortified enclaves. Each side promotes its own view of history. The Greek Cypriot version has had more publicity. and is certainly much better known. President Denktash in the North finds it necessary to give a history lesson first to every new foreign visitor.

Putting aside for the time being the merits of each side's interpretations, it is necessary to present some basic facts about the modern history of Cyprus that would appear to be universally acceptable.

The Greek Cypriots have a longer history in Cyprus than the Turkish Cypriots. Greek speakers began to arrive about 1300 BC. Despite a number of conquests, and a long period of oppressive rule by the Latin Lusignan dynasty and then by Venice, Greek language and culture have persisted in the island. Unlike the Lusignans and Venetians, the Ottomans when they conquered the island in 1571, also deliberately colonised it. They obliged carefully selected peasant farmers and a variety of tradesmen and their families to emigrate from Turkey as colonists. Some Ottoman soldiers also settled in the island, taking local wives. At that time Turks could have equalled in numbers the Greek Cypriot population in an island ruined and depleted by war. They settled everywhere in the island save in the Troodos Mountains. The Greek and Turkish Cypriot communities had their separate villages, or parts of them, and lived apart without much friction. Each community practised its own religion, not intermarrying. Both suffered under the inefficiency and corruption of the later Ottoman regime.

The Ottoman Government, following its normal practice, allowed the leaders of the Greek Autocephalous Eastern Orthodox Church to manage the affairs of the Greek Cypriots for the most part and abolished the serfdom to which they had been subjected by the Lusignan rulers. The Church, despite close Latin control, had kept the Greek tradition alive and has single-mindedly promoted it in modern times. In 1821 sympathy developed in the island for the Greeks in their struggle for independence, with the result that, on what seems to be slender evidence, the Greek Orthodox Archbishop and other prelates were executed.

The next important event was the arrival of the British in 1878. They administered the island on behalf of the Ottoman

Sultan until they annexed it in 1914. British sovereignty was later accepted by Turkey and Greece in the Treaty of Lausanne (1923). Before long the British had to cope with Greek Cypriot demands for *enosis*, union with Greece. Until Cyprus came to be regarded as a vital British base, the British were not unsympathetic, even offering the island to Greece in 1915 if Greece would take up arms against Bulgaria. By 1888, the Greek Cypriots were the majority in the island (74%) and developed a strong campaign for self-determination and *enosis*. They made their point dramatically in 1931 when a mob burned down Government House. The Turkish Cypriot community opposed the Greek Cypriot demand for *enosis* from the very first. They also came under the influence of the new Turkish nationalism developing in Turkey under Atatürk's leadership; they began to demand modern leadership to replace control through the conservative Ottoman elite favoured by the British.

In the 1950s the demand for *enosis* really took hold, especially when the young priest, Michael Mouskos, was elected Archbishop Makarios. Violence against the British began in 1955, led by a Greek Cypriot born Greek Army colonel, George Grivas. The British had a colonial struggle for independence on their hands. They took effective action against the insurrectionaries under the leadership of the Governor, Sir John Harding, and exiled Makarios, who had condoned the violence, to the Seychelles. Less resolute policies thereafter led to Turkish fears that Britain might in the end give up the island. To a degree the British alerted the Turks to the situation in order to counter the Greek Cypriot demands for self-determination and *enosis*, but Turkish public support for the Turkish Cypriots had been manifest since 1949. It was restrained by the Turkish Government as long as Britain's hold on the island seemed secure. After 1955 determined intervention by the Turkish Government reflected pent-up Turkish public feeling.

The British refused Greek Cypriot demands, and would not agree to the division of the island (*taksim*) that was the most popular Turkish and Turkish Cypriot solution. On self-determination, the British Colonial Secretary, Alan Lennox Boyd, declared in the House of Commons in 1956 that 'any exercise of self-determination should be effected in such a manner that the Turkish community should be given freedom to decide for themselves their future status'. In 1958 the policy was reaffirmed by the Prime Minister, Harold Macmillan. The Turkish Cypriots hold the Lennox Boyd statement close to their hearts still.

The British, as a last rather desperate effort, advanced in 1958 the Macmillan Plan, a partnership plan that principally provided for a Greek and a Turkish official to work alongside a British Governor. It was anathema to Makarios; the last thing he wanted was Turkish involvement in the island's governance. Supported behind the scenes by the United States, Greece urged Makarios to accept, instead, an independence solution, without *enosis*. He accepted it reluctantly, Grivas with even more reluctance. Ankara abandoned partition as a solution. But how would an independent regime be structured? The answer was not long in coming, and in a dramatic way.

After an inconclusive Cyprus debate at the UN in December 1958 the formidable Turkish Foreign Minister, Fatin Rüştü Zorlu, uncharacteristically approached his Greek counterpart, Evangelos Averoff, in a friendly way suggesting they should themselves meet to discuss Cyprus in its larger aspects and avoid the wrangling over little points. Averoff agreed. Discussions went ahead. In due course both governments became involved. The British Government was left out, though intimated, when approached, that it did not object to talks about independence. The British had meanwhile come with difficulty to accept for themselves that they could be content with bases in Cyprus, not Cyprus as a base. The Greek-Turkish talks reached fruition in Zurich.

Zorlu and Averoff came to London more or less to tell Britain how it was to give up its own colony. A Treaty of Alliance and a Treaty of Guarantee were proposed; the basic elements of a constitution for the new Republic of Cyprus had been drawn up. The British were to settle the question of bases with the Cypriots, but it was understood there would be British bases. The Treaty of Guarantee was very important. Under this treaty, signed by the new Republic of Cyprus with Britain, Turkey and Greece, both *enosis* and partition were banned. The 'guarantor powers', Britain, Greece and Turkey also guaranteed 'the state of affairs established by the Basic Articles of the Constitution'. They agreed, if the terms of the treaty were breached, to consult about what should be done, whilst recognising that any one of the guarantor states could if necessary take action 'with the sole aim of re-establishing the state of affairs created by the treaty'. The treaties were signed in 1960. The Treaty of Guarantee was invoked by Ankara to justify military intervention fourteen years later.

The fate of the 1960 Settlement

The 1960 Constitution was curious in many ways, being an original creation, not a copy of some other state's constitution, or inspired by some other example. Most significant was that it could not be changed in essentials without the agreement of the external guarantors, which was implied if not stated. Makarios had unwillingly to approve it in 1960, but hoped to change it. The Greek Cypriots complained that Cyprus should have the right to alter its own constitution, or else it was not properly sovereign.

The Constitution did not work well. It has often been described as a 'disguised' or 'functional' federation since it had no geographically distinct constituent entities. The Greek Cypriots generally assert that it provided for a unitary state, the Turkish Cypriots that it was a partnership state. It would be more accurate to say that it was unitary in some respects, but that primarily it was a partnership state in that it required both sides to agree major policy matters. This was to require unanimity, which is the key characteristic of a confederation. It was federal in providing a range of functions for independent communal chambers: they had independent, not decentralised, powers over religious, educational and municipal matters and the right to raise personal taxes.

The restraints on its functioning primarily as a unitary state were that, in a basically presidential system, the Turkish Cypriot Vice-President, like the Greek Cypriot President, had veto powers over important matters in foreign affairs, defence and security. This was not only over decisions of the executive Council of Ministers in these issues, but also over the laws and decisions of the elected House of Representatives! Moreover, legislation in the important areas of the municipalities and the electoral law, or any law imposing duties or taxes, required separate majorities of the representatives elected by the Greek and Turkish communities. (There were separate communal electoral rolls for members of the House of Representatives and for the presidency and vice-presidency.)

Deep disagreement arose over a number of important issues. The Turkish Cypriots wanted less communally integrated army units, and refused to give up the independent powers of their municipalities. The President was also accused of acting high-handedly in foreign affairs and of filling posts with former EOKA members. The Greek Cypriots resented that 30 per cent of administrative posts had to be occupied by Turkish Cypriots. They also wanted to remove the independent Turkish Cypriot municipalities, guaranteed though they were in the Constitution. The crisis came when the Turkish Cypriot members of parliament, as a reprisal for disregard of their interests, refused to vote in a tax law. Makarios declared the Constitution to be unworkable. The Greek Cypriots found it very difficult indeed to accept that the Turkish Cypriots, only 18 per cent of the population, should have virtual equality. The Turkish Cypriots did not trust the Greek Cypriots not to try to overpower them and were therefore suspicious of every Greek Cypriot move. Taking a stand on the majority principle, Archbishop Makarios proposed thirteen amendments to the Constitution that would in effect have turned the Turkish Cypriots into a political minority. Turkey formally rejected the proposals immediately in its capacity as a guarantor power. So then did the Turkish Cypriots, having previously objected informally.

Through its ambassador in Nicosia, Britain seemed to favour the proposed changes, thereby inaugurating a long period of support for the Greek Cypriots which continues to this day. The Makarios proposals were advanced at a time when the moderate Greek Prime Minister, Karamanlis, had been forced to resign and when the Menderes government in Turkey had been overthrown in a military coup. Moreover, the Makarios proposals chimed in with a plan to use intimidation, if necessary, to oust the Turkish Cypriots from their equal role in government. This was the now famed Akritas Plan, a plan to force the Turkish Cypriots into submission, and to declare self-determination as a precursor to *enosis*. It was drawn up by leading *enosis*-minded Greek Cypriots with the approval, and perhaps with the help, of Makarios. Its existence has not been denied by the Greek Cypriot Government.

Its aim was, firstly, to convince world opinion that the 1960 settlement was unjust and unreasonable and that the Turkish Cypriots were intractable and, secondly, to show that the Treaty of Guarantee was therefore an intrusion into Cypriot affairs, and should be annulled. (This would prevent any legitimate Turkish intervention). Thirdly, it was then intended to amend the Constitution without Turkish Cypriot agreement, and finally, to suppress quickly and forcefully any opposition by the Turkish Cypriots before any international intervention could be organised. If Turkish Cypriot opposition created incidents or clashes, then an immediate counter attack on the Turkish Cypriots had to be made, and opposition suppressed with force in the shortest possible time, with the aim of preventing outside intervention. The Greek Cypriots have asserted that a captured Turkish Cypriot plan showed their intention to set up a separate state and divide the island, but examination shows that it was a defensive plan. The Greek Cypriots also believed that the Turkish Cypriots were being trained by Turkish officers and were being supplied with arms. Despite the rejection of partition, the Turkish Cypriots were generally satisfied with the 1960 settlement since it had gone a very long way to meet their claim to political equality.

The outbreak of violence

On 21 December 1963 armed plain clothes Greek Cypriots, claiming to be police, created an incident that led to the killing of two civilian Turkish Cypriots and the serious injury of one Greek Cypriot. It was the beginning of a planned attack on the Turkish Cypriot population designed to intimidate them as intended in the Akritas Plan. The Turkish Cypriots responded with equal violence, being in part prepared. Makarios chose the moment to declare the Treaty of Guarantee null and void, but later had to retract the statement. Turkish civil servants refused to attend their offices, out of fear for their lives, they claimed. The Greek Cypriots' view is that this was part of a deliberate Turkish Cypriot intention to establish their own regime. The violence did not subside. All out Greek Cypriot attacks on Turkish Cypriot areas followed. Turkish planes buzzed Nicosia in protest. British troops had to be called in to try to keep the combatants apart. They established the now famous Green Line in Nicosia which became a border between the Greek and Turkish Cypriot sectors in the capital. The 950 strong Turkish military contingent, allowed under the 1960 treaties, occupied part of the Kyrenia-Nicosia road. Violence erupted in many parts of the island. The Turkish Cypriots sustained many casualties; some 400 were killed, but their resistance was not broken. The Akritas Plan had misfired. At a hastily convened London conference Glafcos Clerides nevertheless called for the recognition of Cyprus as a unitary state, with a common electoral roll, and with minority rights for the Turkish Cypriots. The meeting ended in deadlock.

As mentioned earlier, in Cyprus large numbers of Turkish Cypriots fled to armed enclaves, constituting some 3 to 4 per cent of the total island territory. It is probable that about 40 per cent of the Turkish Cypriot population stayed and lived under Greek Cypriot rule, though their allegiance was clearly to the Turkish Cypriot administration that was soon established in the 39 enclaves, of which the chief was that of Nicosia.

Greek Cypriot rule
Makarios was prepared to have UN, but not NATO, forces replace the British to help keep order. In March 1964 the UN Security Council accepted the request for a UN force from the then purely Greek Cypriot government, referring to it in its Resolution 164 as the 'Government of Cyprus', though not as the government of the 'Republic of Cyprus'. The Turkish Cypriots protested vigorously, seeing the danger that it would be taken to mean the 'Republic of Cyprus', as it later was. The Turkish Government pointed out in a letter to the UN Secretary-General that the only government of Cyprus was that formed in accordance with the Constitution, and containing Turkish Cypriot members. The British Government expressed its agreement and drew the attention of an unsympathetic Secretary-General, U Thant, to the matter. It was to no avail. The Turkish Prime Minister was also apparently persuaded that it was more important to stop the fighting by getting in the UN force than to quibble about constitutional points. The dire result for the Turkish Cypriots was that the wholly Greek Cypriot government came to be regarded by the international community, save for Turkey, as the legitimate government of the Republic of Cyprus.

It was a big step by Britain and the United States along the road of placating Makarios out of fear for the security of the British sovereign military bases and other leased sites on the island. There was also the chiefly American concern that Cyprus should not become a second Cuba. Makarios had not been slow in making approaches to the Soviet Union.

Despite the presence of the UN force (UNFICYP), between 1964 and 1967 attacks on Turkish Cypriot enclaves developed apace under the leadership of Grivas, who had returned to the island to command the Cypriot Defence Forces. By this time more than 10,000 Greek troops had been introduced into the island to augment the 950 allowed under the 1960 Treaty of Alliance. Amongst the many attacks on the Turkish Cypriots those of Kokkina-Mansoura (August, 1964) and Kophinou and Ayios Theodoros (November, 1967) stand out. During the Kokkina-Mansoura fighting, Turkish planes bombed military targets. In 1967 Turkey planned a sea-borne landing, ignoring President Johnson's curt letter to the Turkish Premier, İsmet İnönü, in June 1964 warning against a projected landing by Turkish troops. In 1967 Ankara took a firm line and obtained under threat of intervention, the removal of over 10,000 Greek troops, though some remained, and the raising of the blockade on the Turkish enclaves. Turkey and Greece were on the brink of war. Under a new government Greece drew back. The Turkish Cypriots showed their intentions by establishing the Provisional Cyprus Turkish Administration.

In 1968, as a result of co-operation between Greece and Turkey, and with the help of the UN, talks on revising the Constitution got under way between Clerides and Rauf Denktash, then President of the Turkish Communal Chamber. Serious concessions were made by the Turkish Cypriots under the influence of a Turkish government that wanted good relations with Greece and Europe. They were persuaded to abandon, for instance, their veto rights, but they were loath give up central control of Turkish Cypriot local government, against the advice of the constitutional expert appointed to advise by the Turkish Government. They would also not agree to any overall scheme for change unless there were new assurances that *enosis* would never be proclaimed. This was not possible for Makarios. He was faced with insistent demands for *enosis* by Greek Cypriot opponents supported by a new and more aggressive Greek junta in Athens. Turkish Cypriot resolve was also stiffened by the coming to power in 1973 in Turkey of Bülent Ecevit, who proclaimed that what was needed in Cyprus was a federation.

Turkish military intervention

In July 1974 Makarios was overthrown by troops who supported the Greek junta. He escaped probable assassination and was flown out of Cyprus in a British helicopter. The junta set up Nicos Sampson as the new president, a man hated by the Turkish Cypriots for his notoriously vicious and remorseless attacks on them. The obvious intent was to declare *enosis*. Ecevit flew to London to try to persuade the British Government, headed by James Callaghan, to intervene. In constant contact with Henry Kissinger, the American Secretary of State, Callaghan declined to help to restore the situation to that of 1960, as allowed under the terms of the Treaty of Guarantee. Ankara then went ahead on its own, landing its troops in Cyprus in July 1974.

Some Greek Cypriots believe that Henry Kissinger engineered the coup that overthrew Makarios in order to bring about Turkish intervention and the division of the island between two reliable Cold War allies. It is asserted, not without some truth, that Kissinger made little attempt to stop the Turkish action, unlike President Johnson in 1964. In demonstrations in Nicosia shots were fired at the American Embassy, one of which killed the American Ambassador. The accusation of American masterminding of the 1974 events has been difficult to prove. In refutation, it has been claimed that the American administration was at the time too

A Living History

much involved with the Watergate affair to pay all that much attention to Cyprus.

The first phase of the action resulted, after fierce fighting, in the capture of a small section of the north of the island, including Kyrenia. During a cease-fire, negotiations involving Britain, Turkey and Greece foundered on a Turkish demand for separate self-governing cantons for the Turkish Cypriots, which was a departure from the 1960 Constitution. The Greek Cypriot negotiator, Glafcos Clerides, wanted 48 hours to consult and consider. Ankara feared that prevarication and delay would be used by the Greeks to turn the world against them, and was alarmed by the attacks being made on Turkish Cypriots, particularly in Famagusta. Another factor was that the Turkish troops were in increasing danger of being hemmed in and forced on to the defensive. Ankara refused any delay and demanded immediate acceptance of its terms. This was generally regarded as very unreasonable and evidence of the Turkish intention to capture a large area of Cyprus, if only for bargaining purposes. This the Turkish military then proceeded to do, taking over 37 per cent of the island. World opinion turned against Turkey.

Some 150,000 Greek Cypriots fled to the south of the island fearing what the Turkish army might do to them or to avoid the fighting. Between 40,000 and 50,000 Turkish Cypriots in the south fled to the north, some via the British bases, where they had taken refuge. Others moved as a result of agreement between the Turkish Cypriot and Greek Cypriot sides in negotiations held in Geneva, though that this was ever a formal exchange of populations is denied by the Greek Cypriots. Some 20,000 Greek Cypriots who had been either unable or unwilling to flee to the south of the island remained in the Karpas peninsula under the control now of the Turkish Federated State of Cyprus, soon established in the north of the island. Over the years, restricted in their freedoms, but not persecuted, by the Turkish Cypriot Government, they have nearly all moved to the South. Only about 450 remain.

In the years immediately after 1974 large numbers of Turks emigrated to Northern Cyprus working the lands left by the Greeks and occupying their property, as did the Turkish Cypriots who had fled from the South. By 1983 negotiations through the UN seemed to be making no progress, and the Greek Cypriots under Greek influence, were becoming more hostile and intent on internationalising the issue. In response the Turkish Cypriots declared themselves independent by vote in their elected national assembly and renamed their Turkish Federated State the Turkish Republic of Northern Cyprus. The constitution of the new republic differed little from that of the Federated State and was later approved by over 70 per cent of those voting. The new republic was denounced by the UN Security Council. Britain took the lead in arguing that the declaration of independence contravened the 1960 treaties. The Security Council deplored 'the purported secession' of part of the Republic of Cyprus and regarded the declaration of independence as legally invalid. It called upon all states not to recognise any other Cypriot state but that of the Republic of Cyprus. Only Turkey recognised the new republic.

Aftermath
Since 1974 the new state in the north has suffered considerable economic hardship, mainly as a result of international compliance with the Greek Cypriot claim that direct commerce in any respect with the TRNC would be illegal and would amount to recognition, against the resolution of the UN Security Council. All states, save Turkey, respect this embargo. The greatest economic potential for the TRNC lies in international tourism, but this is essentially prevented by the refusal of international airlines, in support of the embargo, to fly direct to the Turkish Republic of Northern Cyprus. It is mainly through international tourism that, since 1974, the Greek Cypriots have become rich.

Since 1974 the Greek Cypriots have prospered greatly, managing the influx of refugees with great skill. Their state has produced a number of skilful political leaders, quite outshining the less well-endowed North, where their invaluable and only outstanding leader, Rauf Denktash, would be very hard to replace. It was said by Henry Kissinger of Makarios that 'he was too big for such a small island', but it could as well be said of Rauf Denktash.

There has been little violence on the island since 1974. The main incidents have been demonstrations by Greek Cypriots on the border in Nicosia. In 1989 a number of Greek Cypriots, including clergy, and over a hundred women, were arrested by the Turkish Cypriot authorities when they tried to cross into the North. They were imprisoned for a few days and fined. More seriously in 1996 a large demonstration, in which foreign motor-bikers were involved, led to the killing of two Greek Cypriots, one of whom was shot whilst climbing a flagpole to remove a Turkish flag. One Turkish soldier was later killed, and another seriously wounded in what appeared to be reprisal attacks .

A worrying development in recent years has been Greek Cypriot rearmament, put in train out of fear, it is claimed, of Turkish attack on the South. The Turkish side has seen it as an attempt to escalate the conflict in order to attract international attention to the dispute. The programme of rearmament has included importing Russian and other heavy tanks, and the conclusion with Greece of a Joint Defence Doctrine, which has resulted in the establishment of an air base at Paphos. Most important, however, was the plan announced in January 1997 to import Russian ground to air S-300 missiles. This greatly alarmed Turkish public opinion, more perhaps than was strictly necessary considering the range of the missiles. A variety of threats were made in a number of quarters in Turkey to remove them if they were installed. In the upshot, under international, mainly American, pressure, it was decided in late 1998 that they would be installed in Crete. Tension is also kept high by the military exercises that each side holds from time to time.

During the 1990s Turkey showed its unwavering support for Northern Cyprus in a number of joint declarations of solidarity and support. The Turkish Grand National Assembly in a Resolution on Cyprus on 21 January 1997 declared: 'The world must know the fact that the Turkish Grand National Assembly and the Turkish nation are in full unity on this national cause'.

Conflicting readings of history
Greek Cypriot views: From the account given above both sides often select what is important for their case, thus making historical perceptions weapons in their struggle. For the Greek Cypriots the essential point is that they have in modern times constituted a large majority on the island, and that they should therefore rule it on the basis of self-determination, as other former colonial states have done. Appropriate minority rights would be available for the Turkish Cypriot minority. In the general Greek Cypriot view, the British were mainly responsible for the denial of *enosis* and brought in the Turks to bolster their position. The independence plan was essentially forced upon them by agreement between Greece and Turkey. It was a deal that reflected Turkish strength: the 1960 Constitution gave the Turkish Cypriots much more than they deserved. Even so they were not satisfied and wanted a division of the island, refusing to give up their separate municipalities. Their lack of co-operation in many fields made the 1960 Constitution unworkable. They deliberately abandoned their government offices in 1963, creating a crisis that brought in Turkey. In their absence from their government posts the Greek Cypriots had no option but to carry on. They had to make amendments to the Constitution, and take over the government completely. This accorded with the well-known legal doctrine of necessity. Essentially, the Turkish Cypriots are rebels.

Between 1967 and 1974 the Turkish Cypriots refused a new settlement, persisting again on maintaining central control over local government, against the advice of a constitutional adviser appointed by the Turkish Government. After a change of government in 1973 Turkey became more aggressive and seized the opportunity of the Greek junta's coup against Makarios in 1974 to invade the island. This robbed thousands of Cypriot citizens of their land and homes. They were then illegally transferred to many thousands of Turkish immigrants and to Turkish Cypriots. Also there are some fifteen hundred persons missing since 1974, for whose disappearance the Turks are responsible. Turkey now occupies 37 per cent of the island without legal warrant, and controls the North in every way. The Turkish Cypriots are fellow Cypriot citizens, but are now few in number by comparison with the majority of immigrants from Turkey, on whom Denktash and the nationalist government rely for their support. It is not the Turkish Cypriots who are the enemy, but Turkey, which has proved it has aggressive ambitions in the region. The Greek Cypriots are essentially struggling to have their rights lost in 1974 restored to them. A settlement with the Turkish Cypriots will probably have to be in the form of a federation, unwelcome though that is to many Greek Cypriots.

Turkish Cypriot views: The Turkish Cypriots believe that it was always right that they should be treated as a separate community, bearing in mind that the Ottoman Empire owned the island from 1571 and colonised it. They are also very different from the Greek Cypriots in language, religion and culture. There is no single Cypriot identity.

During British rule they declined in importance because the British favoured the Greek Cypriots, feeling more akin to them culturally. When *enosis* raised its head they protested vigorously and eventually the Turkish Government came to their aid. With British indifference, they were treated by the Greek Cypriots as if they were second class citizens. During the violence after 1955 they were the only element in Cyprus on which the British could rely and constituted the bulk of the police force. They gave up their aim of partition, accepting in good faith the independence solution. The 1960 Constitution was essentially a partnership between the two communities, but one which the Greek Cypriots were determined to overthrow. In 1963 the Greek Cypriots put in train the Akritas Plan which initiated a violent attack on the Turkish Cypriots to force them to accept minority status. There were many hundreds of Turkish casualties. It was due to Greek Cypriot terrorism that they had to live in armed enclaves, existing under the blockades imposed upon them only with Turkish assistance. The UN did the Turkish Cypriots a great injustice by accepting the government of the Greek Cypriots as the legal government of the Republic of Cyprus. For the West the Turkish Cypriots were just pawns in the struggle against the Soviet Union. They could be, and were, sacrificed.

After 1964 Grivas returned to lead more vicious attacks on the Turkish Cypriots in their enclaves. They could not return to their government offices out of fear for their lives. When they asked to return to the House of Representatives in 1965, they were told by Glafcos Clerides that they could only do so only if they agreed to changes in the electoral law that would effectively have turned them into a minority. The major Guarantor Power, Britain, did little or nothing to help them, refusing to intervene though it had the legal right to do so. They realised they could rely only on Turkey. In 1974 the Greek junta's aim was *enosis*, in which event the Turkish Cypriots would have been reduced to a minority in a combined Greek state. After Turkey's military intervention, all 45,000 Turkish Cypriots were only too glad to move to the North. The great immediate benefit of the events of 1974 was that the Turkish Cypriots now felt safe for the first time since 1963. More generally, they gained the freedom to determine their own future, a right that no liberal democrat can possibly deny. The Greek rejected equal partnership and will always strive to have the upper hand. They propagandise without any respect for the truth. For instance, Turkish immigrants in the North are not in a majority, numbering at most 40-50,000, and nearly all of them are now Turkish Cypriot citizens. Also there is amnesia on the Greek Cypriot side. It may be that the Turkish Cypriots cannot forget what happened between 1963 and 1974, but the Greek Cypriots cannot remember.

In sum, it may be said for both protagonists that the events in history, and the injustices suffered, are etched deep into their minds. They are a living part of the present problem.

| 3 |

The UN as Broker

The UN Security Council began to try to solve the problem soon after it virtually created it in March 1964, with its Resolution 186, when it chose to recognise the wholly Greek Cypriot government as the Government of the Republic of Cyprus. Its most notable early involvement occurred between 1967 and 1974, when, as has been noted, the two sides came close to agreement on a solution that would have removed the more or less equal political status the Turkish Cypriots enjoyed under the 1960 Constitution.

Immediately after the military intervention of 1974, the UN Security Council tried unsuccessfully to stop further strife. After the fighting was over the UN brought the two sides together in negotiations. The real starting point, however, for a reconciliation of the two sides was the January 1977 agreement between Makarios and Denktash, (who took the lead in arranging it). The two leaders agreed on the following four principles, which are reproduced verbatim since reference is constantly made to them; they are seen as the point from which all negotiations must start. They are:

1. We are seeking an independent, non-aligned, bi-communal Federal Republic.
2. The territory under the administration of each community should be discussed in the light of economic viability or productivity and land ownership.

3. Questions of principles like freedom of movement, freedom of settlement, the right of property and other specific matters, are open for discussion taking into consideration the fundamental basis of a bi-communal federal system and certain difficulties which may arise for the Turkish Cypriot community.

4. The powers and functions of the central federal government will be such as to safeguard the unity of the country, having regard to the bi-communal character of the State.

Federation and confederation

Negotiations thereafter hinged on these principles, but led to differing interpretations of them, especially of points 3 and 4. The Greek Cypriots have claimed the freedoms of movement, settlement and property. The Turkish Cypriots have insisted that these matters should be left to detailed discussion after a settlement. The Greek Cypriot side has also emphasised the need for a wide range of central federal functions to safeguard the unity of the country. The Turkish Cypriots have stressed the bi-communal nature of the proposed state. They have gone further in calling for the recognition of the communities as states. The Greek Cypriots have asserted that there are communal zones, not states, with no real border between them. In the four principles 'federal' was not defined, and there has been surprisingly little discussion on what sort or sorts of government it describes.

The Turkish Cypriots began with proposals for a settlement that interpreted federation as more confederal than federal. They wanted equality in participation in a federal government with few central federal functions, and with residual powers resting with the governments of the two communities. This would have produced a system more confederal than federal. At this stage, it is necessary to state what is generally meant by confederation and federation. Both sides, and the UN Security Council, are reifying these concepts, seeming to assume that they are set in concrete.

Too legalistic an approach to these issues would seem to be partly responsible.

Usually confederation comes about when two or more independent states agree to the joint exercise of power in defined areas of government, as, say, in foreign affairs, defence and economic regulation. In principle all the participating states have to agree on policies in these selected areas, though in less than vital matters there is usually some opting out, or even some majority voting. These two options may be seen in the European Union, which is still mainly confederal in spirit. In a confederation secession is always theoretically possible since sovereignty clearly remains with each state. For major decisions unanimity is the rule.

Representatives of each state forming a confederation may meet to discuss and decide particular matters, or there may be a council made up of representatives of each state. The administration of decisions, and the application of legislation, are usually undertaken by each state, but there may be a joint administration responsible to a central confederal body. An instance of confederation is that of the West Indies, where it was felt that the federation first established after colonial rule was too binding an arrangement for the constituent states.

The boundary lines between confederation and federation can become blurred in practice. The definition of federation is not difficult, though in practice federations differ one from another. One definition by an authority on federation, Daniel Elazar, states simply that it 'is a combination of self-rule and shared rule'. More legal definitions, which are popular in the Cyprus dispute, would see federation as emerging out of agreement by a number of states to divide sovereignty between a central federal authority and the constituent states, with neither usurping the authority of the other. Since on this sort of definition sovereignty is divided, it is not easy to assert that a federation has a single and indivisible sovereignty, as has been asserted in some UN Security Council resolutions on a proposed federation for Cyprus.

There are basically two versions, or models, of federation, though variety is everywhere evident. In the first model the more important governmental functions are performed by federal institutions that are formed by, and are responsible to, the combined electorate of the federated states, not to the individual constituent states, as would be the case in a confederation. This federation arises out of a general cross-state desire to achieve a common goal, as say the popular desire in the early United States to create an American nation. Or it may arise from a demand for economic unity for the sake of economic efficiency. Or there may be a general desire for a political programme or ideology, as in the case, say, of socialism. However, in a federation, outside an agreed framework of central functions, the constituent states remain free. They normally choose to retain important educational and cultural functions, for instance.

A further development of these arrangements, the second model, adds a measure of control by the constituent states over the central, and universally elected, legislature and/or executive. This can be achieved by having a second, or upper, house in the legislature formed by representatives of the states. Its major purpose is to approve, reject, or amend federal legislation. This would normally be achieved by a majority vote of the constituent states' representatives, as in the American Senate. In this way the states as a whole, though not individually, act as something of a check on the federal centre, which is responsible primarily to the electorate as a whole. In this composite type of federal state, most power normally resides in the generally elected body, but it will be appreciated that it is virtually impossible to say where sovereignty lies. Much the same may be said of so-called unitary states when they are liberal and democratic in structure. In such states there is usually some significant division of powers between and among the legislature, the executive and the judiciary. In political reality, as has been pointed out by another authority on federalism and federation, Preston King, the dividing line between a federal state and a liberal and democratic unitary state can be very indistinct. The formal and traditional classification of states as 'unitary,' 'federal' or 'confederal' does not withstand close scrutiny.

Both the unitary and the federal forms of state can be difficult for a minority community to accept, especially if there are only two significant communities, as in Cyprus, with one much smaller than the other. This is why the Turkish Cypriots, whilst using the language of federation, have always in fact wanted confederation. When their early formulations in this direction made no progress in the UN sponsored negotiations, they accepted that the federal centre would have important functions, but only on condition that any major legislation or acts of government were subject to a veto by either community. This was to repeat the spirit and form of the 1960 Constitution, which allowed a veto to each community's representatives in the institutions of government in vitally important areas.

The Draft Framework Agreement, 1984-1986
Early proposals from the Turkish Cypriots for a very loose form of federation were turned down by the Greek Cypriots. There was deadlock until the two leaders, Spyros Kyprianou and Rauf Denktash, met in May 1979 to agree on ten points that included making the Makarios-Denktash guidelines, and relevant UN resolutions, the basis of further talks. In 1984 the then UN Secretary General, Perez de Cuellar, drew up a draft constitution for agreement, known as the Draft Framework Agreement. The Turkish side accepted it. At first it seemed to have Greek Cypriot support, but unexpectedly, in December 1984, it was rejected by the Greek side. They also rejected a revised version in 1986, although that too was accepted by

the Turkish Cypriots. The latter could accept the UN
formulations because they provided for major matters of
legislation to require separate majorities of deputies in both
chambers of a bi-cameral legislature. Moreover both the
Greek Cypriot president and the Turkish Cypriot vice-
president, could veto a long list of major areas of legislation
and of executive decisions, a longer list than in 1960. The
Greek Cypriots did not make much comment on these
constitutional matters. They turned down the 1986 Draft
Framework Agreement because it did not address itself
directly and unambiguously to the three freedoms of property
ownership, residence and movement, the removal of foreign
troops, the return to Turkey of the thousands of 'settlers' in
the North from Turkey, and the reinstatement in the North of
the 150,000 or so Greek Cypriot refugees. The Turkish
Cypriots had also only gone as far as to offer to withdraw to
29 per cent of the territory of the island from the 37 per cent
they held. The rejection of the solution by the Greek
Cypriots, led by President Kyprianou, who was closely
supported by the Greek Prime Minister, Andreas Papandreou,
was a great disappointment for the UN Secretary-General and
the UN, especially in view of Turkish Cypriot acceptance *in
toto*. The rejection produced political turmoil in the South,
where parliament and people seemed ready to accept the
solution proposed. The Greek Prime Minister's support was
crucial for Kyprianou's victory.

The 'Set of Ideas', 1992
In a new formulation of proposals in 1992 by the then
Secretary-General, Boutros Boutros Ghali virtually the same
provisions for veto were repeated that were contained in the
Draft Framework Agreement. (See Appendix 1.) Each
community's representatives in the lower house of the
legislature could decide that in certain important areas of
government they could choose to require a majority of votes
from each community's representatives. The areas of

government concerned can hardly be considered unimportant: foreign affairs, defence, security, budget, taxation, immigration and citizenship. In those same areas the president and vice-president also, conjointly or separately, had the right to veto any law or decision of the legislature, or any decision in these areas of the executive Council of Ministers. In other words unanimity between the two sides was required in major matters, both in legislation and in executive decisions, but unanimity, it will be recalled, is the hallmark not of federation, but of confederation. It is odd that when in 1998 the Turkish Cypriot Government announced, with the support of the Turkish Government, that they wanted a confederation, the UN Security Council condemned a principle that in reality had lain behind the proposals advanced by the Secretary-General, with the full support of the UN Security Council, in 1984-86, and again in 1992. It might be argued that, technically, the UN Security Council would have to turn down confederation because confederations are formed by independent states, and the TRNC is not a recognised state. On the other hand it is normal for federations to be formed by independent states too.

In 1992 the Turkish Cypriots agreed to 91 of the 100 UN proposals. However, they wanted a rotating presidency, equality in the Council of Ministers, the rotation of ministers, the removal of economic disparities between the two states, and the retention of 29 plus per cent territory, which was more than was envisaged in a draft map submitted by the Secretary-General.(See Appendix 2.) They also wanted strict conditions for the return of Greek Cypriot refugees that made their return look well-nigh impossible. The Greek Cypriot side did not commit itself, not being under much pressure from the UN Security Council to do so. They advanced proposals for the legislature and executive that did not admit of a veto power. They accepted the UN proposals as a basis for reaching an agreement, subject to negotiations that would accord with international law, human rights and the 'functionality of the state', but Boutros Ghali realised that there would be serious difficulties on their side: there were too many provisos. The Turkish Cypriots were said by the UN Secretary-General to be 'outside the framework of the 'Set of Ideas', though they had agreed to most of them. They had not anyway previously committed themselves to staying within the UN parameters.

Troutbeck and Glion negotiations
In 1997 the UN tried once more to bring the two sides together. Meetings were held in Troutbeck (New York) in July and in Glion (Switzerland) in August. The tactic adopted by the UN Secretary-General differed from that in 1984-86 and in 1992. Instead of proposing a constitution, the UN Secretary-General tried to persuade both sides to agree on a broad set of principles that would provide the basis for a constitution. This was a brave attempt to reconcile the irreconcilable. There were difficulties from the outset, especially over where sovereignty would be located in the new state to be established. The Greek Cypriot side objected strongly to the UN suggestion that sovereignty 'emanates equally from the Greek and Turkish Cypriot communities'. There was a storm of protest in the Greek Cypriot press, all the major party leaders condemning the idea. Also how could it be said that sovereignty was 'indivisible' if in the last resort it rested in each community? Other similar bones of contention arose. Political equality it was said, 'shall be reflected in the *effective* participation of both communities in all organs and decisions of the federal government' (italics added). It was soon pointed out that 'effective' does not mean 'equal'.

At the second meeting in Glion the UN altered its second Draft Joint Declaration mainly in favour of the Greek Cypriot side, dropping the shared sovereignty idea. This displeased the Turkish Cypriots, but any hope of agreement had been dashed by the announcement by the European Union towards the end of the Troutbeck meeting that the EU would go ahead with accession negotiations with the Greek Cypriots. This prompted Denktash to say that he was only going to Glion to make the point that he could not participate in any meaningful way if the TRNC was not recognised as equal. There was no result from Glion. The UN Security Council blamed the Turkish Cypriots for the failure. 'There was a sense that commendation was due to President Clerides for the flexibility and co-operation he had shown...[and] there was some concern and disappointment that further substantive progress at this time was impeded by the attempt to bring preconditions to the table by the other party, and here I mean, of course, the Turkish Cypriots'. This precondition was, of course, non-acceptance of the government of the Republic of Cyprus as the rightful government of all Cyprus. The Turkish Cypriots' riposte was that the UN's acceptance of the legality of the government of the South as the Government of the Republic of Cyprus was the real precondition.

The TRNC was fully supported by the Turkish Government. Ankara had learned by then that it was very unlikely to be included as a candidate for the next EU enlargement. Between Troutbeck and Glion, Turkey and the TRNC, in a Joint Statement, announced that the two states would pursue a policy of integration in the spheres of economy, finance, defence and foreign affairs, with a Joint Council to implement the agreement. Clerides described this development as 'irresponsible'.

Turkey's policy of support was enhanced by the EU's December 1997 European Council decision not to include Turkey among even the slow track aspirants to EU membership. Turkey's aspirations were generally recognised, but were said to depend *inter alia* on support for a Cyprus solution based on Security Council resolutions. That Turkey was held responsible for good relations with Greece and for progress on Cyprus were much resented in Turkey. The Government declared it would not discuss Cyprus further with the European Union.

Confidence-building measures
The failure of the 1992 'Set of Ideas' initiative impelled the UN Security Council to try to promote in 1993 and 1994 a set of confidence-building measures between the two sides. Welcoming them at first the Turkish Cypriot subsequently had second thoughts, having noted some serious disadvantages in the scheme. The main idea was for the area of Varosha on the east coast, a decaying tourist centre, to be ceded to the Greek Cypriots in return for the reopening of Nicosia Airport for joint use. The scheme came to nothing because of fears by the Turkish Cypriot side that they would be surrendering some of their best bargaining counters, and because the Greek Cypriot side believed that the scheme would give a degree of recognition tothe North. The Turkish Cypriots did in the end propose amendments to the original scheme that were acceptable to the UN Secretary-General, but the South had by then come to believe that its main objectives could be better attained by persisting with its application for membership of the European Union.

New York and Geneva (1999-2000)
The UN tried again to bring about reconciliation by arranging a series of proximity talks starting in December 1999. A call for renewed negotiations had been made by the G8 group of seven industrialised countries plus Russia. The UN Security Council responded on 29 June (Resolution 1250) calling for negotiations with no preconditions [to stop the North demanding recognition] and with all issues on the table [to make it clear to the South that confederation might be discussed]. The two sides were to negotiate through the Secretary-General until a settlement was achieved and with full consideration of relevant UN resolutions and treaties

[presumably the 1960 treaties of Alliance and Guarantee]. The first round of these proximity talks began in December 1999 in New York. The second round was held in Geneva in the following January and February, the third round in Geneva in July, the fourth round in New York in September and the fifth round in Geneva in November. A sixth round was scheduled for January 2001 in Geneva, but after consultation with Ankara Denktash decided not to attend

These proximity talks were designed to be exploratory, intending to find common ground. They were subject to a news blackout, but in response to some provocative comments made by Denktash, Clerides took the opportunity to state that for him the object of the talks was not to create a new state, but to amend the 1960 Constitution, to make it federal rather than unitary. He ruled out confederation as not providing the necessary single sovereignty and common citizenship. It has been noted earlier that this sort of legalism is unrealistic and unlikely to lead to a solution. It has also been argued above that in reality it is very wide of the mark to believe the 1960 Constitution established a unitary state (if this sort of terminology is to be retained). As has been argued earlier, its dominant characteristic was power sharing and, for the most part, it was confederal in spirit.

More important than this skirmish were the confidential 'non-documents' presented to both sides at the fifth round by the Secretary-General, Köfi Annan, but of which extracts (or perhaps all) were somehow obtained by the Greek Cypriot press. They contained alarming propositions for the Turkish Cypriot side. Principally they outlined a presidential type federal system that allowed for a bi-cameral legislature, along the lines of the Greek Cypriot submissions during the 1992 'Set of Ideas' negotiations. The lower house would be elected by the populace as a whole, with some reserved seats for each community, but decisions would be by majority voting with no veto for the deputies from each community. The upper house was to consist of an equal number of members from each community. It could reject legislation by majority vote, as in the American Senate, but again there was no provision for a communal veto. Also Greek Cypriot domination of the executive (the Council of Ministers) was apparent. It is not easy to understand why such a proposal was made, unless it was thought that with Turkey at last *en route* to the European Union after Helsinki, and eager to join, some pressure could now be exerted on the Turkish Cypriot side.

Under pressure though Ankara was by the end of 2000, the Turkish Government rejected any suggestion that the Cyprus issue could be linked with its bid for EU membership. It was behind Denktash when he said he would only attend more UN negotiations if they were on a new basis that paid heed to the sovereignty and equality of the Turkish Cypriot people. In line with this position Lefkoşa now considered refusing to allow the UN Peace Force (UNFICYP) to operate in the North without its specific permission. Freedom to operate had already been restricted, and payments for certain services in the North had been demanded. The Turkish Cypriot Government objected strongly that the UN asked permission for UNFICYP only from the Government of the Republic. On 16 December the TRNC Legislative Assembly declared that the process of proximity talks had lost its meaning and that it saw no purpose in continuing the process.

By the end of January 2001, however, it seemed that Ankara was hoping that talks could be resumed. The possibility of a Palestine-type formula was being mooted. It would provide for territorial sovereignty, but not for an independent state.

It is clear that developments in the European Union with respect to both Cyprus and Turkey are having profound effects on the UN's role in the conflict. The 'catalyst' is at work, though the results may well not turn out to be those that were expected five years ago.

| 4 |

The EU Catalyst

The relations of Cyprus with what is now the European Union began in 1961 shortly after Britain's application was made. The motive was economic. Commonwealth preference would end if Britain's application was accepted; the market of the then Six was also important. This economic motivation led eventually in 1972 to an Association Agreement with the European Communities. The Turkish Cypriots did not benefit much from financial and other aid subsequently delivered, save in the early years between 1974 and 1978. Later they participated in a funded joint sewerage scheme in Nicosia. There was supposed not to be any discrimination between the two communities, but financial aid went almost exclusively to the South. This was because the Turkish Cypriots refused to submit projects through the Cyprus Central Bank, in order to avoid recognition of the 'illegal' regime in the South.

The Association Agreement with Cyprus consisted of two stages and provided for a customs union to be completed in fifteen years. A customs union is not as satisfactory as full membership of the European Union. It opens up the local market to EU competition, but denies access to structural funds and to economic policy making. Also it covers only industrial, not agricultural products, which is not advantageous for less industrialised countries. Nor does it allow free movement of labour. The economic benefits of membership, over a customs union, are substantial, but the discipline of EU membership was also in some ways economically disadvantageous. It was really for political reasons that the Republic of Cyprus applied in 1990 for full EU membership.

A good deal of the impetus came from Greece which, in 1981, had become a member of the European Union. At first the then Greek Cypriot president, George Vassiliou, was cautious. He depended a good deal on AKEL which strongly favoured non-alignment and was not sympathetic to the European 'rich man's club'. The Greek socialist premier, Andreas Papandreou, was determined, however, to find a favourable solution to the Cyprus problem by internationalising it. His actions in this regard encouraged the Turkish Cypriots in 1983 to declare their state to be the Turkish Republic of Northern Cyprus.

The EU followed UN practice by not recognising the TRNC, accepting that the Republic of Cyprus was entitled to sovereignty over the whole island. The Greek Cypriots believed that if the application succeeded, it would show that Turkey was occupying territory within the European Union and would reinforce the view that Turkey was responsible for the Cyprus issue. Membership of the EU would also deter Turkish aggression, it was thought in the South, though whether Turkey would ever attack the South without provocation must be regarded as very doubtful, despite large numbers of Turkish troops in the North. It would be a major diplomatic blunder very difficult to justify to the international community.

With Greek assistance the Republic's application moved fast. In 1993 the EU issued an Opinion on the application. It was inaccurate as to the North, and biased in favour of the Greek Cypriots. The North had certainly refused to co-operate in what it regarded as an illegal application, but there is much published statistical and other information available in print that could have been used. The Republic was regarded as eligible for membership, but it was also stated that accession was conditional on a settlement of the dispute. If the inter-communal talks failed it was decided to reassess the situation in 1995 in the light of the positions adopted by each side. The June 1994 Corfu European Council, whilst noting that Cyprus was to be involved in the next enlargement, still pointed to the need of a settlement. This position was endorsed by the British Prime Minister in the House of Commons, when he stated that Cyprus was very far from accession due to a difference between the Greek and Turkish Cypriots. Nevertheless, during this period before talks began in earnest, the EU was generally coming down on the side of the Greek Cypriots. This was signified in 1994, as mentioned earlier, when the European Court of Justice in effect banned the importation into EC countries of citrus fruit and potatoes. This was a substantial blow to the economy of the North, already held back by the international embargo.

In January, 1995, the European Commission reviewed the holding decision it had made in 1993 on the accession of Cyprus. This was after receiving a report from its observer, Serge Abou, also the author of the Opinion. The report noted that there was little hope of a settlement and put the blame mostly on the Turkish Cypriot side, with many plaudits for Mr Clerides' courage and open-mindedness.

The EU might have been minded to wait further, but in March 1995 was manoeuvred into agreeing to a date for the beginning of accession negotiations with the Republic. This occurred because Greece was threatening to veto the conclusion of a customs union with Turkey unless a date was given for negotiations to start. The conjunction between these two events is routinely denied. The EU made a virtue out of necessity by claiming that the accession negotiations would be a 'catalyst' to solve the Cyprus problem. In Turkey the political opposition argued that Ankara could have backed away from the Customs Union, to prevent the EU from agreeing to open accession negotiations. In the Turkish parliament tempers were frayed. Turkey seemed to have reneged on its promises to maintain the Turkish Cypriots' 1960 treaty rights. The Government denied this, claiming that the EU would have agreed to the beginning of accession negotiations for Cyprus anyway. Greece could certainly have threatened to veto EU enlargement to the East, but this would have been much more difficult than to veto a none too popular EU-Turkey customs union, since the eastern expansion was greatly favoured by Germany.

Ankara, and the Turkish Cypriots, claimed, and still maintain, that the 1960 treaties forbade the union of Cyprus with any other state, and that, as a member of the EU, Cyprus would be in union with a number of them, including Greece. Also in Article 8 of the Basic Articles of the 1960 Constitution, which, under the Treaty of Guarantee the Republic undertook to respect, it is laid down that the President and Vice-President each has the right to veto any law or decision concerning foreign affairs, 'except [those allowing for] the participation of the Republic in international organisations and pacts of alliance in which the Kingdom of Greece and the Republic of Turkey both participate' (Articles 50 and 57 of the Constitution). The legal opinion sought by the EU argued that as no vice-president now existed, the provisions of the 1960 Constitution dealing with the vice-presidency were presently inoperative.

Some EU member states expected that the March 1995 package deal would induce Greece and Turkey thenceforth to be more amicably disposed to each other. However, both sides denied that it was a package deal, assumed no responsibility for the outcome, and showed no signs of greater amicability. Nor did they assume in 1995 that accession negotiations would not be linked to a solution of the Cyprus problem. The French Foreign Minister, Alain de Juppé, who masterminded the March compromise, made it clear that the French understanding was that Cyprus meant a federal Cyprus.

In the years after 1995 some member states of the European Union continued to express doubts about the accession of the Republic of Cyprus without a settlement on the island. The EU therefore came to believe that a way to bring about a settlement would be for the Turkish Cypriots to participate in the accession negotiations with the Greek Cypriots. After some hesitation the Greek Cypriots declared that they would accept Turkish Cypriot representatives alongside them, but only if they recognised the legitimacy of their 1990 application to join the European Union. It seems that some EU states hoped and expected that Turkish Cypriot participation would encourage a solution, or would, at least, encourage the emergence of some agreements in, for instance, economic matters, as a way of bringing the two sides together. It was not apparently intended that the Turkish Cypriots would have a veto on any decisions. This initiative was really to grasp at the last straw, however. The Turkish Cypriots could hardly be expected to enter into such negotiations save as members of an equal and recognised state. They pointed out that their acceptance of the invitation in the form presented would be tantamount to recognition of the 'illegal' government of the South. It is a little difficult to understand how the British Foreign Secretary, Robin Cook, could seriously claim that Clerides' willingness to accept Turkish Cypriot representatives was 'a genuine and realistic offer'.

Recent Greek-Turkish relations
The events of March 1995 brought the TRNC and Turkey closer together. The reconciliation hoped for between Greece and Turkey did not materialise. There was little chance when, with a change of government in Ankara, Mrs Çiller was replaced as prime minister by Necmettin Erbakan, head of the anti-European Islamic party: he had been in coalition with Ecevit in 1974 when Turkey intervened in Cyprus. In June 1997 a new government headed by Mesut Yılmaz, with

Ecevit as coalition partner, was, if anything even more supportive of the North, if clearly pro-European Union. Also elections in the South (1990) and the North (1998) showed continuing solid support for their leaders, so there was no reconciliation apparent on the island. In fact the situation deteriorated badly in 1996 when, as mentioned earlier, Greek Cypriot demonstrations on the border led to the deaths of two Greek Cypriots, and later to two casualties on the Turkish Cypriot side. In January 1966 a dispute over the ownership of a rocky island, Imia/Kardak, close to Turkey in the Aegean, nearly led to a war that was averted by the intervention of the US President and his emissary, Richard Holbrooke. More was to come. In January 1997 the South announced it was purchasing S-300 surface to air missiles from Russia. Various threats to remove the missiles were made in Turkey. A sea and naval base was also being constructed in Paphos in the South under the Greek-Greek Cypriot 'Defence Doctrine', a mutual defence arrangement made in 1993. Exercises by the armed forces of Greece and Turkey close to Cyprus have also created tensions that could ignite a spark. The South meanwhile, is spending large amount on rearmament, to which Turkey has apparently responded by increasing its military strength in the North.

Tensions were reduced somewhat when at a NATO meeting in Madrid in July 1997 the Greek Prime Minister, Costas Simitis, and the Turkish President, Süleyman Demirel were induced to sign an Accord denouncing the threat or use of force. This declaration, and co-operation in NATO between Greece and Turkey, both under moderate leadership, helped keep the situation stable.

It continued to be hoped that with the EU's agreement to a firm date for Cyprus accession negotiations, and with the Turkish Customs Union in place, relations between Turkey and Greece would improve. There have been some encouraging signs, though Turks are sceptical about permanent improvement in relations. With many others they tend to assume, and not without evidence, that embedded in the Greek mind is a deep traditional dislike of Turks. As Ottomans they had destroyed the Byzantine Empire, the repository of Greek civilization. Also the Greeks had fought a bitter national war of liberation against the Ottomans in the early nineteenth century. The Turks have reciprocated this dislike, but to nothing like the same extent.

Against this background it has been difficult to come to agreement on two major sources of conflict between them, the Aegean and Cyprus. In the former case Greece believes it has the legal right to extend territorial waters around its numerous Aegean islands from six to twelve miles. Turkey has declared this would be a *casus belli*, since it would seriously limit Turkish movements in the Aegean, almost two-thirds of which would come under Greek control. Greece has also claimed offshore mineral rights in the Aegean. Greek claims are for about two-thirds of an area that is unlikely to turn out to be rich in oil, but where there may be additional claims made for adjacent sea and air space.

There are those in Greece, in governmental, educational, journalistic, and business circles who are not hawkish about Turkey, and not even about Cyprus. More surprising is that in August 1999 the government and the people of Greece responded with considerable sympathy and generosity to Turkey's earthquake disaster. Turkey responded in similar vein when an earthquake occurred in Athens the following month. Also in 1999 the Greek and Turkish foreign ministers began a dialogue on bilateral issues. The removal in 1999 of Theodore Pangalos, the Greek foreign minister regarded by Turkey as aggressive and anti-Turkish, was also welcomed in Ankara.

By 2000 relations between Greece and Turkey were better than for a long time, so that there is more hope that the two governments will be able to influence the protagonists in Cyprus to make allowances for each other's demands.

Turkey and the EU

Turkey's relations with the EU dropped to a new low in December 1997 when it was made clear in the Luxembourg European Council, after months of suspicion, that Turkey was not in fact to be included even among the slow track applicants to the Union. Particularly galling to Ankara was that the strengthening of Turkey's links with the EU would *inter alia* depend on Turkey's establishing satisfactory relations with Greece and on supporting the UN-aided negotiations on Cyprus, the clear implication being that Turkey did not do so. Turkey refused any further discussion with the EU on these and other matters until rather more considerate attitudes began to appear on the EU side.

Finally, in Helsinki, in December 1999, the European Council formally accepted Turkey as a candidate for membership on a par with the other twelve applicants. Along with all candidates, Turkey was urged to make every effort to resolve outstanding border disputes and other related issues. There was also reference to an enhanced political dialogue with Turkey with particular reference to border disputes, and other related issues, and for the UN Secretary-General's efforts to bring the Cyprus proximity talks to a successful conclusion. After some hesitation, these terms were declared acceptable by Ankara, though Turkey was apparently still held responsible to some degree for a settlement. Greece supported this new stance by the EU, perhaps aware that it is more likely to weaken Turkish resolve to support the TRNC, than hostility. The Greek Cypriots were reassured, moreover, by the statement that whilst a settlement would facilitate the accession of Cyprus, it was not a precondition. They were less reassured by the Council's intention to 'take account of all relevant factors' in coming to its decision. The Council's stance removed any possibility of a Turkish Cypriot veto, but the mention of a settlement and consideration of 'all relevant factors' does continue to worry the Greek Cypriots. Every EU member state has eventually to approve the Cyprus application for membership, and some of them continue to express deep misgivings about its accession without a prior settlement.

For Turkey there was a hiccup with regard to Cyprus in the long-awaited EU's Accession Partnership document for Turkey (8 November 2000). Among the short-term goals (i.e. for 2001) was an open and more specific call upon Turkey 'to support strongly in the context of the political dialogue, the UN Secretary-General's efforts to bring the process of finding a comprehensive settlement of the Cyprus problem to a successful conclusion'. Ankara objected to what it saw as a reversion to pre-Helsinki attitudes. In consequence the EU General Affairs Council in Nice in December agreed to preface the quotation above with 'in accordance with the Helsinki conclusions' and to add to the end, 'as referred to in Point 9(a) of the Helsinki conclusions'. Point 9(a) referred to the EU's strong support for the UN Secretary-General's efforts to bring the negotiations to a successful conclusion. Despite these amendments, there is still a good deal of feeling in Europe that Ankara holds the key to the Cyprus dispute.

The EU in Cyprus
Whilst the UN was proceeding with its abortive negotiations, and after Holbrooke's vain efforts to bring about an agreement, the EU sought to influence the situation by making EU membership for the island seem irresistible to the Turkish Cypriots. A representative in Cyprus was appointed, with the title of Ambassador, to promote the EU cause. A good deal of information on the benefits of EU membership was distributed in the North, until the TRNC Government banned it. Some visits to Brussels for Turkish Cypriots were also arranged. On a larger scale were American efforts to bring together groups from each side, building people to people contacts. The American Special Co-ordinator for

Cyprus, Thomas Miller, claimed that 600 meetings had been promoted with 2000 participants.

Richard Holbrooke had also been instrumental in aiding this economist policy by bringing together Greek and Turkish businessmen with their counterparts from South and North Cyprus. All this seemed to the North to constitute an attempt to undermine the loyalties of its own populace, to substitute economics for politics, on the dubious grounds that wealth is more important than political freedom, and would be the way promote a solution. Other groups claimed to find much mutual sympathy between ordinary citizens from both sides and made the point that it was only the political elites that were driving Cypriots apart, forgetting, perhaps the strength electoral support on both sides for their leaders. In December 1997 meetings across the border were banned by the Turkish Cypriot authorities, though the left-wing political parties continue to meet quite frequently.

In attempting to persuade the Turkish Cypriots that membership of the EU is highly desirable the EU would seem, at first blush, to have some chance of success. A reliable poll in 1997 showed that 95 per cent of Turkish Cypriots wanted to join the EU, though, it must be noted, 84 per cent only after a solution of the Cyprus problem. Moreover, half of these would only want to join if Turkey joined at the same time. Turkish Cypriots are sensitive to the advantages of economic development because, perhaps, their own economy has expanded discernibly in the last few years.

This modest taste of prosperity must help make Turkish Cypriots more eager for material betterment. It was, therefore, not welcome when lax governmental control resulted in a Turkish inspired economic austerity package in the summer of 2000. Schemes to make public utilities pay their way, the taxing of pensions, and increases in other taxes led to the quite large recent demonstrations in 2000 mentioned earlier. The Greek Cypriots have taken great heart from these expressions of dissatisfaction. They renew their call to ordinary Turkish Cypriots to join with them as compatriots in a new political comradeship, now hopeful that they will force their political leaders to change course. They do not propose political equality to the Turkish Cypriots, however, and they tend to overlook the hard political fact that in the 1998 parliamentary, and the 2000 presidential, elections, the nationalist right was more popular than ever.

Solutions and the EU
From the EU's perspective a federation with a strong set of central institutions and functions would probably be the best form of government for accession. There would be a strong and coherent government to accept and administer, at least, legislation and decisions emanating from Brussels. A more confederal system would be more difficult unless, say, an appointed Joint Council was given very large functions, including economic policy. In both cases, and certainly in the case of a federation that recognised Greek Cypriot pre-eminence, the Turkish Cypriots would be in a very weak state within the institutions of the European Union. They would certainly feel the need to have Turkey there to help them.

Another solution sometimes advanced would be for the two Cypriot states to enter the European Union separately. Provided there was some prior agreement on the proper border between them, this would seem to be a practical way to proceed. The prohibiting factor is that the EU, following the UN, only recognises one sovereign authority in the island and will presumably do so for a long time to come. A variation on this scenario, should it ever be considered, would be for the South to enter first, to be followed by the North at a later date.

The major difficulty in all these scenarios is that the Greek Cypriots have always demanded freedom of movement, residence, and the right to buy property in the North, as part of the whole island. In any solution, federal or confederal, in essence they would expect these three freedoms to be regarded as natural rights available to themselves as to all members of the European Union. The Turkish Cypriots would want these rights to be restricted by derogations, like those that exist elsewhere in the European Union, as in Denmark and Finland (for the benefit of the Swedish speaking community). In so electric a political atmosphere as Cyprus, however, there would no doubt be perpetual pressures on the EU by the Greek Cypriots for recognition of the temporary nature only of any such derogations. In any settlement the Turkish Cypriots would no doubt require that the derogations they would find necessary should remain in force without question until Turkey also became a member state of the European Union.

The freedoms the Greek Cypriots want for Cyprus are part of the essence of membership of the EU and account for much of Greek Cypriot desire for Cyprus to become a member. In March 1998, at the launching of the accession negotiations with the eleven new applicants, including Cyprus, the British Foreign Secretary reminded them that all member states have to honour the resulting rights and obligations of membership, including free movement of goods, services, capital and persons. Transitional measures, he reminded them, must be limited in time and scope. This is just what the Greek Cypriots want to hear.

For the Turkish Cypriots it would seem wisest, assuming these general attitudes to prevail, to join the European Union, if at all, alongside Turkey. If that should come about it might well then be the Greek Cypriots who would be looking for derogations to prevent the 65 million Turks on their doorstep from taking advantage of EU rights of domicile and investment. The Greek Cypriots could come to rue the day they applied for EU membership as a way to help solve the Cyprus problem in their favour.

The EU's engagement in accession negotiations with the Republic of Cyprus has altered the whole Cyprus scene. It has added a complexity some observers believe the Cyprus problem did not need. Cyprus does not have any substantial economic gains to make from joining the European Union and its membership confers no benefits on the European Union. The Turkish Cypriots believe that without the imprimatur of acceptance by the European Union, the Greek Cypriots would doubtless have become less confident about their legal rights, and political legitimacy, and consequently would have been more inclined than they are now to come to some compromise agreement. In their turn the Greek Cypriots believe that, but for Turkish support, the Turkish Cypriots would have agreed to compromise.

The withdrawal of all international influences, including that of the UN, has been urged by some, but it would only be possible if the two sides were equally balanced. The Turkish Cypriots feel they would be too weak to defend themselves against Greek Cypriot aggression without Turkish help, but Turkish support is seen by the Greek Cypriots as a threat to their security: They know they cannot fight Turkey with any hope of success. Intervention by the UN could hardly have been avoided, but there has to be a large question mark over EU involvement. It has certainly added to the complexity of the conflict. Sensible counsels clearly exist in Europe, but the rules of the EU have allowed the Greek side to advance its cause. This has been a remarkable achievement by Greece, at least in the short term. Whether there will be a boomerang effect only time will tell.

| 5 |

Cyprus and the World

The Near and Middle Eastern world on which Cyprus immediately impinges has a fragile stability, and sometimes not even that, as the Israel/Palestine problem shows. This stability is vital not only to the West, but to practically the whole world. This is because, together with the Caspian region, it has great reserves of oil, presently a major and indispensable source of energy, until it is replaced, safe nuclear, and/or some other sources of energy. Hence the need for stable and co-operative regimes in this area of the world. This means the containment of basically unstable and dangerous regimes, like that currently in control of Iraq. Hence, too, the need in particular to ensure that relations between a mainly Muslim Middle East and the Christian, or post-Christian West do not become permanently hostile, as could become the case.

These concerns of the post Cold War world, which showed how real they were in 1990 with the Gulf War, mean that it is vital that Turkey continues to see its future as part of the western world in general, and of Europe in particular. For Turkey is in immediate proximity to the Caspian and Middle Eastern regions, and possesses very substantial and efficient armed forces backed by a large and rapidly developing economy. In addition, Turkish society is in general Islamic, even though the state struggles, so far successfully, to remain mainly secular. Turkey is disinclined to play a prominent role in the Middle East, but has the power to do so if need be. In this regard it is not unimportant that its control of water sources gives it influence over Syria and Iraq. It also has arrangements in the military sphere, in areas of supply and training facilities, with Israel. Turkey is also particularly close to Turkish-speaking Azerbayjan, an important source of oil production, and seeks close relations with the Turkic-speaking new states of Central Asia, with whose peoples the romantic national right in Turkey feel an empathy, even if it is not always reciprocated.

Without the present use of İncirlik airbase, in particular, it would be impossible to enforce the ban on Iraqi flights over northern Iraq. It is also important that a major oil pipeline route is planned to go through Turkish territory to Ceyhan in South-east Anatolia.This partly accounts for the Turkish military's belief that it might well need to have a permanent base in Northern Cyprus, especially if relations with Greece do not improve and Greece maintains a base in Cyprus. Other, and cheaper, pipe-line routes maybe used for the transportation of Caspian oil, but it is realised that they could be less secure than the route to Ceyhan.

The United States, as the world power, is more aware than is the European Union of the economic and military importance of Turkey to the Middle East, the Caspian and Central Asia. Hence the pressure that is said to have been put on the European Union to be more forthcoming about Turkey's possible membership of the European Union. In Europe, Turkey is seen primarily as an economic and social problem with important implications for the enlargement of the European Union. There are also major worries within the European Union whether Turkey can satisfy the Copenhagen criteria. These worries include political and human rights, minority rights for the Kurds, the curtailment of military influence in government and efficient administration. For the EU, Turkey is not yet seen as a strategic asset, though the realisation of Turkey's importance in the Eastern Mediterranean seems to be on the increase. What has brought Turkey's importance home to European states has been Turkey's proximity to, and influence on, the Balkans in recent years.

The United States

To the United States Cyprus is in itself of relatively minor importance and Greece is less central to its concerns than Turkey. Nevertheless, the Cyprus issue is still important if it should lead to Greek-Turkish hostility, or, worse, conflict, in the Eastern Mediterranean, even though it is not as important now as it was during the Cold War. However, this is not to say that Cyprus is without strategic importance. To the Americans the British sovereign bases on the island are significant for storing American material and as staging posts for any conflagration that may occur. The United States must also benefit from the areas in the Troodos mountains leased for use as listening posts. There is also a Greek lobby in the United States that, from time to time, has caused difficulties for the American administration with regard to Turkey and Cyprus if the American administration seems to be taking too Turkish a line. It is not surprising, therefore, that the United States, despite numerous assertions of the importance of a solution in Cyprus, has tended not to come to the forefront. If there is no threat of a Greek-Turkish conflict, or threats to the British bases, there is no need to do so. When the United States has intervened in recent years, as most notably with Richard Holbrooke's mission, it has kept firmly within UN guidelines. Holbrooke was careful to maintain American recognition of the Greek Cypriot Government as the government of the island, though on occasion intimating that he recognised the factual existence, at least, of the Turkish Republic of Northern Cyprus. Significantly Holbrooke's emphasis came to be placed on developing economic and business contacts between the two communities, not on trying to broker the political settlement that is crucial.

The United Kingdom

The British approach has much in common with the American, or perhaps it should be put the other way round. Britain still plays a major role in the Cyprus dispute by virtue of being a Guarantor Power under the 1960 treaties, and on account of the sovereign base areas. Britain is also a permanent member of the Security Council and advises the UN Secretary-General in important ways. Britain's special representative on Cyprus is Sir David Hannay, who was appointed in May 1996. He had been Britain's Permanent Representative in Brussels and Ambassador to the United Nations in New York and is the most prominent of the many national representatives; he also represented the EU during the Luxembourg presidency (1998).

Britain is not greatly trusted in the North. The Turkish Cypriots do not forget (since both sides are immersed in their pasts) that although a Guarantor Power, Britain chose not to support the Turkish Cypriots during the fateful years from 1963 to 1965: Britain did not intervene effectively to save their position under the 1960 Constitution. In 1983 Britain promoted the Security Council resolution which called on all states not to recognise the new Turkish Republic of Northern Cyprus. The Turkish Cypriots are aware that the British Labour Party now in power has always been sympathetic to the Greek Cypriot cause, a sympathy stretching back to support for self-determination for Cyprus under a Greek Cypriot majority in Makarios' time. Britain is also not trusted in the South, if not to the same degree. It is alleged that Britain has virtually condoned the Turkish 'invasion' of 1974 by inactivity and lack of real commitment to support for a government it recognises to have authority over the whole of the island. Britain is also not regarded as a particularly strong power and does not receive the respect accorded to the United States.

The major British concern has to be the maintenance of their bases and of listening posts elsewhere in the island leased from the Greek Cypriot Government. The bases are officially described as valuable for training, aerial reconnaissance, logistics and storage of equipment. Britain also has to bear in mind that there are some 20,000 British civilian residents in the South, by comparison with only three to five hundred in the North. The largest single group of the two million tourists who each year visit Cyprus is British.

Any difficulties that should be created by the Greek Cypriots with regard to the bases might well, of course, affect the numbers of British tourists to the South (very few go to the North, which does not provide much popular tourism). If the South entered the EU without an agreement, it might well be argued by some in the South that the 1960 treaties had broken down through the lack of support of the international community in general and by Britain in particular. This could lead to demands for the surrender of the bases to the Republic. There is already an undercurrent of feeling that they should not exist under British sovereignty. That they are under British sovereignty in what would be geographically EU territory will seem odd, even though the bases are not included in British territory forming part of the European Union. The bases are also pretty much open to access by Greek Cypriots. For Britain it would be more satisfactory if there were an agreed settlement. It is sometimes cynically suggested, however, that the best solution for Britain is perpetual negotiation. Certainly during the past twenty-five years the bases have not been under any serious threat.

Does concern for the bases adequately explain a consistent British policy since 1960 of support for the Greek Cypriots? Certainly during the crucial period after 1960, Britain was under less pressure from Turkey. After the 1960 military coup domestic affairs dominated Turkish politics and the formidable Foreign Minister, Fatin Rüştü Zorlu, was no longer directing what had been a very determined Cyprus policy. With a change of government at that time, Greece also became more supportive of Makarios.

In support of the British position it may be argued that there would have been little point in restoring a constitutional government in Nicosia that would again, no doubt, prove to be 'unworkable' or would be made unworkable. Nor was there any alternative political formula to hand. A geographically based federation was not possible. In 1965 the first UN mediator, Galo Plaza rejected the restoration of the 'oddity' of the 1960 Constitution and proposed minority rights for the Turkish Cypriots. In addition, the governments of the many new states in the post-colonial world would not welcome support by Britain of a Turkish Cypriot minority, lest it set an example for their minorities. Moreover, these new states were numerous in the United Nations General Assembly and had the sympathy of the Secretary-General at the time, U Thant.

There may also be other considerations. The Turkish Cypriots are inclined to believe that the British Government and the Foreign and Commonwealth office have a natural bias in favour of Greeks over Turks, understanding them and the culture they represent better. Also Greek Cypriot, and Greek, publicity and lobbying in Britain for their cause has been extensive and effective.

Other Actors

The other major European states are distinctly uneasy about the prospect of no settlement before Greek Cypriot accession, but have not openly broken ranks, and stand behind the UN Security Council's efforts to promote a settlement without prior recognition of the political equality of the Turkish Cypriots. The British Commonwealth routinely supports the British approach. Many states have minorities that they do not wish to encourage. The Organisation of the Islamic

Conference is also cautious, and whilst expressing wholehearted support for the Turkish Cypriots, has not recognised the Turkish Republic of Northern Cyprus.

In some ways the Council of Europe creates as many difficulties for the TRNC as the European Union, though sometimes it has shown in the past an awareness of the existence of the TRNC. The Council of Europe may have no real power, but it influences opinion in Europe being composed of the parliamentarians of European states. For twenty years after 1964 the Council did not allow a Greek Cypriot to deputise for a Turkish Cypriot. It only did so after the declaration of the Republic in 1983, which it did not recognise, but Turkish Cypriot parliamentarians are allowed to address political groups. This helps understanding the Turkish Cypriot case, but the Council's Court of Human Rights has influenced the Council's other institutions against Turkey and the TRNC. In a case brought by Mrs Titina Loizidou, the Court in 1996 decided that Mrs Loizidou had a right to her property in the North and found that Turkey was responsible for the actions of the TRNC after 1990, the year Turkey recognised the jurisdiction of the Court. The Government of the TRNC was regarded as a subordinate local administration. It is a warning to Turkey and the TRNC to be careful not to promote the *political* integration of the two states, but to insist on their separateness, even though Turkey, because of the embargo, has little choice but to help the TRNC economy. Even emphasis on needed economic measures when instigated by Turkey makes some Turkish Cypriots feel that they are gradually being turned into Turkey's eighty-second province. That Turkish Cypriot vessels will be allowed to fly the Turkish flag and that Turkish citizenship and passports will be made available to Turkish Cypriots underline the dangers of too close an integration.

Without a settlement, and with the accession of the Republic of Cyprus to the European Union, it is often asked what will be the position of the Turkish Republic of Northern Cyprus. The position of the TRNC may well be less difficult than is sometimes suggested. The country is used to getting by and would no doubt continue to develop slowly, with the not altogether water-tight economic embargo being gradually eroded as foreign investment of non-European origin, like that of Israel, is attracted by the possibilities of tourism.

If the Republic of Cyprus enters the EU without the TRNC, a very difficult situation is bound to arise in the Eastern Mediterranean generally. Turkey will be held to be occupying territory that forms part of the European Union, and is in a customs union with the European Union. Turkey will be in the awkward position of recognising both the Republic of Cyprus and the Turkish Republic of Northern Cyprus. The EU might propose sanctions against Turkey, but this could only lead to Turkish withdrawal from the Customs Union. Turkey may be denied any hope of membership of the European Union, but this would only reinforce the Islamic and nationalist opposition in Turkey and would undermine Turkey's position as bridge to, or barrier between, Europe and the Middle East and Central Asia. It would seem certain that, without a satisfactory settlement of the Cyprus dispute, Turkey's entry into the European Union would be blocked by Greece and the Republic of Cyprus. The alienation of Turkey from Europe would not be welcomed by the United States, especially under a Republican administration. If the Republic of Cyprus is to enter the EU in 2003 or 2004 without a settlement, there is now little time to change the existing situation. The EU 'catalyst' has made it very much more difficult to find a solution, but demands urgently that one shall be found.

| 6 |

Is There a Solution?

There are two basic reasons why there has not been a settlement of the Cyprus dispute. The first is that each side believes in its own principles to an extent that compromise looks and feels like surrender. In this respect, and others too, their cultures are similar, but it is not of much help in coming to an agreement. Just the reverse.

To recapitulate on these general attitudes, the first area of disagreement lies in the realm of political theory, or better, perhaps, democratic ideology. The Greek Cypriots stress that they are a majority in the island, still constituting at least three quarters of the population. They must therefore have the democratic right to govern the island, whilst paying respect, of course, to the cultural rights and freedoms of the Turkish Cypriot minority. They feel no hostility towards their Turkish Cypriot fellow citizens who are after all, primarily Cypriots like themselves. They just wish to be rid of the alien Turks who are occupying over two thirds of their national territory.

The second Greek Cypriot argument is historical. The Greek Cypriots unquestioningly regard themselves as having the right to rule the island on the grounds that it has been basically Greek in language and culture for many hundreds of years before the Turks arrived. The Turks are only one of a number of conquerors over the centuries. In the end they have all gone away or have been absorbed into the Cypriot population. The same will happen with the Turkish Cypriots. They will make their own contribution in due course as Cypriots, as, they claim, many wish to do.

The Turkish Cypriot stance is also two-pronged. In 1571 the Ottomans not only conquered Cyprus, they also colonised it. No conquerors before them had done this. They had simply subjugated what was a culturally mixed local population, by no means completely Greek in origin. Unlike previous conquerors of the island, the Ottomans then granted the Greek orthodox population extensive freedoms to rule themselves under their own church leaders, freeing them from serfdom. On account of their different language, religion and culture they did not mix much with the Greek Cypriots, but together with them formed the basic peasant and artisan population of the island. They shared the benefits, and tribulations, of rule by the Ottomans and then by the British. They were only forced into hostility to the Greek Cypriots by the policy of *enosis*. If the Greek Cypriots had not embraced Greek nationalism, and *enosis*, they would have been able to establish a satisfactory partnership with the Turkish Cypriots. The dire events of 1963 to 1974 showed what little respect the Greek Cypriots had for them. The Turkish Cypriots believe that they are not to be trusted.

In these circumstances it was inevitable that the Turkish Cypriots established their own state free from Greek Cypriot domination. Moreover, they argue, any group of people that freely chooses to govern itself has an absolute right to do so. Self-determination is a basic tenet of liberal democracy that no-one can deny. In 1958 the British Government recognised the Turkish Cypriot right to self-determination. There can be no historical, legal or moral justification for not recognising their state. No outside power or international body has any right to presume that they should be in an inferior position to the Greek Cypriots, with whom they are perfectly prepared to share power equally in an island that ought to be united.

As has been mentioned earlier, the UN Secretary-General has in the past tried hard to reconcile these fundamental differences of principle by seeking agreement on 'guiding principles' for a settlement, as in 1992 and in 1997. These brave attempts to obtain compromises on matters of principle, well meaning though they are, actually do more to highlight differences than to remove them. In this regard, it might be helpful if the words like 'sovereignty' were omitted from all future documents.

More concrete issues
The crucial area of dispute in the Cyprus problem is clearly that of creating a political system that satisfies both Greek and Turkish Cypriots. The Turkish Cypriots want political equality: the Greek Cypriots believe that they should be more than equal. The other issues in the dispute are also important, but could be regarded as secondary and easier of solution.

There is, first, the problem of how much territory the Turkish Cypriots should retain. The surrender of the derelict area of Varosha/Marash on the east coast would probably not be at issue. The transfer of Famagusta, an important port for the North, would be of a different order, but some agreement on joint use of the facilities might be possible.

Territorial adjustments in the rather barren central plain would probably cause few difficulties, but the citrus-growing area of Morphou/Güzelyurt is an altogether different matter. In the 1992 map it is shown as ceded to the Greek Cypriots. (See Appendix 2.) Some 7,500 Greek Cypriot owners, or their descendants, could claim the right to return, displacing the present Turkish Cypriot cultivators. They and the very many other Turkish Cypriots now in the area could be re-housed, but probably they would all become refugees in the territory of the North. In 1992 this was not a situation the North was prepared to accept.

The rights of Greek Cypriot refugees from 1974 to return to their former properties in areas to be under Turkish

Cypriot jurisdiction is another problem. These properties now have Turkish Cypriot deeds: after 1974 they were allocated to Turkish Cypriots from the South and to immigrants. The properties have often been improved and some will have changed hands. It has been suggested that not many Greek Cypriots would now wish to return, if it meant living under Turkish Cypriot rule, and would be prepared to accept compensation. Turkish Cypriots would almost certainly not want to return to their former properties in the South. As a solution to the problem, global exchange of properties has been urged in the North and finds some unofficial support in the South. The decision of the Court of Human Rights in the Loizodou case referred to earlier may well have some influence on the situation, but it is not clear what that effect, if any, would be.

The Greek Cypriot demand for freedom of movement between the two federated states would seem to present few problems, provided that those of vengeful or fanatical inclination were restrained. Freedom of domicile, however, could lead to serious diminution of the Turkish Cypriot character of the North. Freedom to invest and to own property might result in economic domination by the Greek Cypriots. If, after a settlement, the island were to enter the EU, permanent derogations would no doubt be sought in these two areas.

Another problem is the reduction of security forces on both sides, but viable ways of achieving demilitarisation would not seem too difficult to contrive

A way ahead?

Can there be some circumvention of the major issues of principle at the core of the dispute? Now, after Helsinki, there will probably be pressures on Ankara to produce concessions from the Turkish Cypriot side. The Turkish Foreign Minister, İsmail Cem, and the Prime Minister, Bülent Ecevit, have both declared that there is no junction between

Turkey's application to join the EU and the Cyprus issue. Leading Turkish newspaper columnists doubt that this position can be maintained. They may well be right, but it is very doubtful that Ankara would, or could, persuade Lefkoşa to compromise on its basic principles of equality and recognition. It may be that the Turkish Cypriot Government could be persuaded, say, to give up some territory and to open up Famagusta as a port to both sides, even if some territorial concessions should uproot a number of Turkish Cypriots, though with generous compensation. These would be important concessions, but they are of a secondary nature as compared with concessions of principle. It is doubtful if any Turkish government could survive that agreed to Turkish Cypriot surrender to Greek Cypriot majority rule. Cyprus has of recent years become a much larger factor in Turkish public opinion that used to be the case, and Turkish security interests over Cyprus have become more pronounced now there is a base there open to Greece.

Is there, then, little or no chance of a solution? Both Sir David Hannay and Richard Holbrooke have seen the 1992 UN sponsored 'Set of Ideas' proposals as offering some hope for the future. Property, territorial, and defence issues, might well be overcome with concessions on both sides. There could be just a possibility that the Turkish Cypriot insistence that they will enter into negotiations as a recognised state might be circumvented. It might just be enough for them if it were made crystal clear in the text of any agreement that they were in fact entering into it as a recognised state. They would then be taking the next step of abandoning that status only for the sake of the formation of a federation.

The issue of a Turkish Cypriot veto over major legislation is very difficult indeed, even though it was provided for in the 1992 'Set of Ideas' and was in line with the principles inherent in the 1960 Constitution. One difficulty of the 1992 proposals was that the federation would have had a very wide range of functions, so that the use of a veto available to either side could well have resulted in the sort of deadlock experienced between 1960 and 1963. Although the Greek Cypriots did not make a large issue of the veto in the 'Set of Ideas' negotiations, they would no doubt have rejected it. However, many of the major policies that in 1992 would have had to be decided by the federal government would be already virtually settled if the federation became a member of the European Union. In the knowledge of what they would anyway have to accept as members of the EU, the Turkish Cypriots might well find that they did not now need such wide veto powers as provided for in the Set of Ideas. Moreover, if the federation could be constructed with a minimum of federal powers, with functions left, wherever possible, to the authorities of each of the two communal states, there would be less opportunity for friction at the centre. Whether there should be at the outset a federal parliament, or a council chosen by both sides, is a matter for serious consideration. So, too, is the extent of representation by each side. In this regard, the more chance the political elites have of working together on serious issues, the more likely are they to be able to develop a consensus on other issues across the communities. Consociationalism might then develop. Without a high degree of consensus, and a genuine desire to make it work, no federation is going to be successful. What seems important at present is first to develop mutual confidence and trust over as limited an area as possible. It is in the necessary acceptance of the *acquis* by both sides in a federation that has some confederal features that the EU 'catalyst' might come into operation. If there is to be an elected legislative assembly, with or without communal vetoes, it might, if unusually, be designed to be equipped for a period with powers over matters that are not likely to be contentious.

For the UN Secretary-General and the Security Council this means that inventiveness and flexibility are the vital qualities needed. Constitutions are not set in stone. Every federation is different. There is no reason why a hybrid system cannot be constructed or, better, be allowed to grow. The Greek and Turkish Cypriots have to be asked whether the constitutional principles they avow are as mutually exclusive as they imagine. The European Union is itself a confederation with developing federal features.

In this flexible sort of scheme the Greek Cypriots may well believe that they would be giving up the essentials of their position. They would, in fact, be agreeing to a large degree of independence for the Turkish Cypriots in a federation, but as the much larger element they could surely afford to do so. If they handled matters with tact and care, there is little doubt that over the years, and within the EU, their influence would increase, or better and more likely, the differences between the two communities would become much less apparent. The Greek Cypriot fear that once recognised the TRNC would simply withdraw from whatever federal or confederal arrangements were agreed is not realistic. It would certainly be a possibility if the Greek Cypriots looked for domination over the Turkish Cypriots. Otherwise the Turkish Cypriots would be very disinclined to take the alternative route of complete integration with Turkey, grateful though they are for Turkish protection. Also, with eyes on Europe, Turkey would be strongly inclined to discourage secession.

There is little time left for a settlement to emerge. The EU will have to come to a decision on the admission of the South, with or without the North, within the next few years. In the conditions of EU politics it may be very difficult for any member state to demand a settlement before the South is admitted. With time pressing, it is a time for statesmanship, not for political and constitutional wrangling, and time to escape the tyranny of words.

Appendix 1

'Set of Ideas', 1992
(Excerpts)

CONSTITUTIONAL ASPECTS OF THE FEDERATION

III. The powers, functions and structure of the federal Government will be in conformity with the overall objectives and guiding principles set out above.

A. *Powers and functions to be vested in the federal government*

The federal Government will have the powers and functions listed below. All powers and functions not vested in the federal Government will rest with the two federated states. The federated states may decide jointly to confer additional powers and functions to the federal Government or transfer powers and functions from the federal Government to the federated states.

The federal Government will have the following powers and functions:

    (a)   Foreign affairs (the federated states may enter into agreements with foreign Governments and international organizations in their areas of competence. The representation in foreign affairs will reflect the bi-communal nature of the federal republic);

    (b)   Central bank functions (including issuance of currency);

    (c)   Customs and the coordination of international trade;

    (d)   Airports and ports as concerns international matters;

    (e)   Federal budget and federal taxation;

    (f)   Immigration and citizenship;

    (g)   Defence (to be discussed also in connection with the Treaties of Guarantee and of Alliance);

(h)   Federal Judiciary and federal police;
(i)   Federal postal and telecommunications services;
(j)   Patents and trademarks;
(k)   Appointment of federal officials and civil servants (on a 70:30 Greek Cypriot/Turkish Cypriot ratio;
(l)   Standard setting for public health, environment, use and preservation of natural resources, and weights and measures);
(m) Coordination of tourism and industrial activities.

The federal powers and functions will be executed by the federal Government or, in accordance with agreements, through delegation to the federated states.

B. *Structure, composition and functioning of the federal Government*

1. *The Legislature*
The legislature will be composed of a lower house and an upper house. The presidents of the lower house and of the upper house cannot come from the same community. The president and vice-president of each house will not come from the same community.
All laws must be approved by both houses.

The lower house will be bi-communal with a 70:30 Greek Cypriot/Turkish Cypriot ratio.

The upper house will be a 50:50 ratio representing the two federated states.

All laws will be adopted by majority in each house. A majority of the Greek Cypriot or Turkish Cypriot representatives in the lower house may decide, on matters related to foreign affairs, defence, security, budget, taxation, immigration and citizenship, that the adoption of a law in the lower house will require separate majorities of the representatives of both communities.

Separate Greek Cypriot and Turkish Cypriot majorities will be required to constitute a quorum in each house. If a quorum is not attained in either house on two consecutive meetings because of the absence of a majority of one or both communities, the president of the relevant house will call a meeting in no less than 5 days and no more than 10 days. At that meeting, a majority of the upper house will constitute a quorum. In the lower house, 30 per cent of the total membership will constitute a quorum.

If the two houses fail to adopt a bill or decision, they will initiate proceedings to obtain a consensus while ensuring the continued functioning of the federal Government. To this end, a conference committee will be established. The conference committee will be composed of two persons each selected by the Greek Cypriot and Turkish Cypriot groups equally from among the members of the two houses of the federal legislature. The text of the legislation or decision agreed to by the conference committee will be submitted to both houses for approval.

In the event the federal budget is not adopted in one or both houses and until an agreement is reached by the conference committee and is adopted by both houses,the provisions of the most recent federal budget plus inflation shall remain in effect.

2. The Executive

The federal executive will consist of a federal president, a federal vice-president, and a federal council of ministers. The president and the vice president will symbolize the unity of the country and the political equality of the two communities.

[On the question of the election of the president and vice-president, the two sides have expressed different positions. The Greek Cypriot side prefers a system under which the president is elected by popular universal suffrage. The Turkish Cypriot side prefers a system under which the president rotates between the two communities.]

To facilitate the effective launching of the federal Government and for the initial eight years, the president and vice-president will also be the heads of their respective federated states.

There will be a council of ministers composed of Greek Cypriot and Turkish Cypriot ministers on a 7:3 ratio. The president and vice-president will designate the ministers from their respective communities who will appoint them by an instrument signed by them both. One of the following three ministries, that is foreign affairs, finance, or defence, will be allocated to a Turkish Cypriot minister. The president and the foreign minister will not come from the same community.

The president and the vice-president will discuss the preparation of the agenda of the council of ministers and each can include items in the agenda.

Decisions of the council of ministers will be taken by majority vote. However, decisions of the council of ministers concerning foreign affairs, defence, security, budget, taxation, immigration and citizenship will require the concurrence of both the president and the vice-president.
Arrangements related to the implementation of foreign policy and the composition of the foreign service will be set out in the federal constitution.

The president and the vice-president will, separately or conjointly, have the right to veto any law or decision of the legislature concerning foreign affairs, defence, security, budget, taxation, immigration and citizenship. The president and vice-president will have the right, separately or conjointly, to return any law or decision of the legislature or any decision of the council of ministers for reconsideration.

3. The Judiciary

The federal judiciary will consist of a supreme court composed of an equal number of Greek Cypriot and Turkish Cypriot judges appointed jointly by the president and vice-president with the consent of the upper house. The supreme court will sit as the federal constitutional court and the highest court of the federation. Its presidency will rotate between the senior Greek Cypriot and Turkish Cypriot members of the supreme court. Lower federal courts may be established in each federated state.

The supreme court will deal with matters arising under the federal constitution and federal laws, and will be empowered to fulfil other judiciary functions related to federal matters attributed to it by the federal constitution or federal legislation.

Each federated state will have its own judiciary to deal with matters not attributed to the federal judiciary by the federal constitution.

The federal constitution will establish the procedure for ascertaining the constitutionality of federal laws and executive acts, as well as adequate machinery of judicial review to ensure the compliance of legislative, executive, and judicial acts of the federated states with the federal constitution.

Appendix 2

Map attached to the 'Set of Ideas'

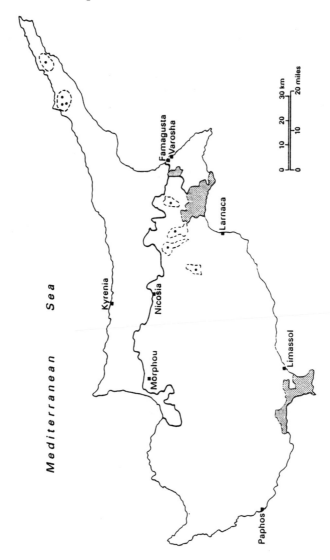

Further Reading

A reading list on the Cyprus problem would take many pages. The following books provide broad coverage.

Antoniou, Andreas; Axt, Heinz-Jürgen; Bağcı Hüseyin; Baier-Allen, Susanne (ed.); Brey Hansjörg; Cameron, Fraser; Couloumbis, Theodore A.; Dodd, Clement; Joseph, Joseph S.;.Larrabee, F.Stephen ; Olgun Mustafa Ergün; Rühl, Lothsar; Sonyel, Salahi R.;Tahiroğlu, Mehmet; Theophanous, Andreas; Ünal, Hasan and Valinakis, Yannis G.
Looking into the Future of Cyprus-EU Relations (Centre for European Integration Studies, Rheinischen Friedrich-Wilhelms-Universität Bonn). Baden-Baden: Nomos Verlagsgesellschaft, 1999.

Axt, Heinz-Jürgen; Bartmann, Barry; Brewin, Christopher; Dodd (ed.), Clement; Ertekün, Necati M.; Lindley, Dan; Olgun, Mustafa E; Sonyel, Salahi R.; Stavrinides, Zenon and Zambouras, Sergios.
Cyprus: The Need for New Perspectives. Huntingdon: The Eothen Press, 1999.

Brewin, Christopher
The European Union and Cyprus. Huntingdon: The Eothen Press, 2000.

Crawshaw, Nancy.
The Cyprus Revolt. An Account of the Struggle for Union with Greece. London: Unwin, 1978.

Dodd, Clement H.
The Cyprus Imbroglio. Huntingdon: The Eothen Press, 1998.

Kyle, Keith
Cyprus: In Search of Peace London: Minority Rights Group
International, 1997.

Sonyel, Salahi R.
*Cyprus. The Destruction of a Republic. British Documents 1960-
65.* Huntingdon: The Eothen Press, 1997.

Stavrinides. Zenon.
The Cyprus Conflict: National Identity and Statehood. 2nd edn.
(with a foreword by Michael Moran) Lefkoşa: Cyprus Research
and Publishing Centre, 1999.